L Crookall

British Guiana

Or, Work and Wanderings Among the Creoles and Coolies, the Africans...

L Crookall

British Guiana
Or, Work and Wanderings Among the Creoles and Coolies, the Africans...

ISBN/EAN: 9783744751698

Printed in Europe, USA, Canada, Australia, Japan

Cover: Foto ©ninafisch / pixelio.de

More available books at **www.hansebooks.com**

BRITISH GUIANA

OR

*WORK AND WANDERINGS AMONG THE CREOLES AND
COOLIES, THE AFRICANS AND INDIANS OF
THE WILD COUNTRY*

BY THE

REV. L. CROOKALL

Author of

"BOOKS: HOW TO READ AND WHAT TO READ," "TOPICS
IN THE TROPICS," ETC.

ILLUSTRATED

LONDON
T. FISHER UNWIN
PATERNOSTER SQUARE
MDCCCXCVIII

CONTENTS.

I.

OFF TO THE WEST INDIES AND THE SPANISH MAIN 1

Sailing out—The mysterious passenger—Adjusting the compasses — Home compasses — Political compasses — Ecclesiastical compasses—Dover from the sea—A "sneezer" —How she fought the storm—A man overboard—A look in at Dartmouth—"Westward Ho!"—My native land, farewell—Struggles within—On to our shelves—A first night at sea—Dinner hour—The doctor, the lawyer, and the parson—"Quite correct, sir!"—What is life?—The Azores—St. Michael's—"Ponta Delgada"—Under the stars in a tropical sea—Orion—Venus and Mars—In the tropics—The melting-room—A whale—Flying-fish—Barbadoes—In Carlisle Bay—Bridgetown—Off again.

II.

GUIANA, OR THE WILD COAST . . . 22

First view of land—Peculiarities of coast—The schoolboy's answer—Derivation of Guiana—When discovered—Visited by Raleigh—El Dorado—Gold and diamonds—Government returns—Situation of the Wild Coast—River Amazon—Orinoco—Its fifty mouths—A curious geographical fact — Divisions—British Guiana—Brief history of

CONTENTS

PAGE

British Guiana—Berbice—Demerara—Essequebo—The three great rivers—The Cuyuni—The Rupununi—The Potaro—Kaieteur Falls—A new world—Population and subsistence—The country's resources—Grand prospects—Its soil—Its productiveness—The farmer's difficulty—Coast lands and interior—Savannahs—Forests—A terrene ocean—Schomburg on these Guiana plains—The great savannah—Supposed site of El Dorado—The Ituni downs—Wild cattle—Tigers and jaguars—Climate—The "Transatlantic Eden"—Temperature—Tradewinds—Purity of atmosphere—Wonderful plants—How to live long.

III.

THE LAND WHERE SUGAR GROWS . . 42

Opinions of Demerara—A warm land—The seasons—The moonlight—Getting moonstruck—Thirteen springs—Thirteen autumns—Strange facts—Queen Luna—A land of equality—The lords of the soil—Days and nights—Trees always green—No winter—A sweet land—Golden syrup—Sweet potatoes—Sweet cassava—Sweet plantain—The saccharine element—A land of exuberant vitality—"Bêtes-rouges"—Frogs—Sandflies—Mosquitoes—The leaf of life—Sugar—Sandvoort village—Orange—Birds—Tigers in town—A savage alligator.

IV.

THE HISTORY OF A POUND OF SUGAR . 56

At the tea-table—Demerara crystals—Fashions—Society—Cane sugar—Its good qualities—It is very ancient—Was grown in Palestine—Estates and plantations—Cane in full bloom—Labourers at work—Mill for grinding—Value of the land—Clearing and draining—Planting—A day's earnings—Ploughing—Weeding—The "Arrows"—Harvest—Cutting the canes—Transporting them to factory—Crushing them—The juice—Boiling them—The vacuum pan—Molasses—Packing and shipping.

V.

IN A TROPICAL HOUSE. 65

Curious noises—Beetles and borers—Frogs and their whistles—The grand concert—The six o'clock beetle—A

CONTENTS

tropical house—Why on pillars?—Jalousies and verandah—Where is your chimney?—Which way to sit—How they cook—Taps and vats—Upstairs—Like a bird in a cage—Mosquito curtains—Vampire bats—Centipedes—Shake the folds of your skirts—It was up my trousers leg—Jiggers—Poking them out— Morning coffee—Song of old Jane—When it is cool—Breakfast—Kinds of fish—Luncheon—Fruit-trees—Dinner—Foo-foo soup.

VI

IN A TROPICAL CITY 77

Georgetown—On river Demerara—The harbour—Water Street—The market—Vegetables, fruits, and flowers—Plantains—Everything different—Like the Tower of Babel—The stores—Dollars and cents—Tramcars—Policemen—The post-office—The museum—The lighthouse—The sea-wall—Main Street—Camp Street—Roman Catholic Cathedral—Brick Dam—The burning bush—Avenue of palms—The Botanical Gardens—Fan palms—The Corypha—Cabbage palms—Royal palms—Coquirita palms—Ita palms—Snow plant—Character d'homme—Lady of the night — Public buildings — Town-hall — Churches and chapels—Pleasures of the city.

VII.

UP TO BERBICE 96

The coasting steamer—Mouth of Berbice river—Crab Island—The old Dutch fort—Canje Creek—The new span-bridge—View of New Amsterdam—The landing—Water Street—Merchant stores—Prices of commodities—Main Street—Rum shops—Peculiar names—Formation of streets—The trenches and bridges—Different races—Occupations — Town council — Town-hall — Court-house — Churches and chapels—Public hospital—Providence estate and Islington—Overwinning—Congo Africans—The old slave's story—The east coast—Scandal Point—Queenstown—Lunatic Asylum—Coolie huts—Sowing the rice—How the coolies live—A coolie family.

CONTENTS

VIII.

IN A TROPICAL CHURCH 116

Religion in British Guiana—Sunday—Service in church—A mission chapel congregation—The people's dress—The queer side of things—The Chinese—Windows and doors—Disturbing noises—Funny habits—Labouring under difficulties—Numerous creatures and insects—"Cockles"—The singing—Bible knowledge of the natives—Faith of the old slaves—Different races worshipping together—Uses of a tropical church — Baptisms of children — Strange names—A tropical wedding—Ludicrous mistakes—"After you, sir!"—Funerals—The suddenness of death—"Watch ye!"

IX.

PARSON AND GORGONZAMBE 132

The old African—Gorgonzambe or God-doctor—A bad mind—An Obeah man—Funny expressions—The chamber of sickness—A parson's work—Hours of consultation—Ballata—Ballata bleeding—Bush adventures—The Indian's petition—The trouble of Mrs. S—— —Mr. K. in court—Another petition to government—The "Act of Verweezing"—Parson's vat—Kindliness—Charles II.'s chaplain—A parson's worries.

X.

THE OLD AFRICANS OF GUIANA . . . 149

Different races—The black people—The negro's story—Introduction of the Africans into British Guiana—Slave days—Horrors of slavery—Cruel punishments—Flogging—The slave-market—Pincard's description of a sale—A mother's anguish—The slave mother's farewell—Condition of the slaves in the early part of this century—Dawn of a new light—Moffat and Livingstone—John Wray—Slaves singing—The old Dutch church—The slaves' hope—"Gingo"—Buckra—The Bible and the rats.

CONTENTS

XI.

EMANCIPATION AND ITS RESULTS 169

The Act of Emancipation—Planters' responsibilities—A slave's daily work—A rumour of freedom—Rising of slaves on La Resouvenir—Rev. J. Smith taken prisoner—A false verdict—Sixty years after—Advancement of the people—Religion to-day—Ecclesiasticism and religion—Government—Medical men—Established churches—The London Missionary churches.

XII.

UP THE BERBICE RIVER 183

Preparations for our journey—The aborigines—His life—His needs and wants—His pictures—Hammocks—Necessary provisions—Starting off—Description of the river—The homa—Lianos—The forests—Savannah—Anchored—Our sleeping place—Meditations—Strange noises—Wild hogs—The Midnight sky—The Southern Cross—Rain and sandflies—Daylight—off again—The old fort—The old Dutch Governor—Jumbies—The chest of gold—Our destination.

XIII.

AT ZEELANDIA 194

The old Dutch plantation—A mysterious light—"Saf'ly ribah run deep"—The Gladstone family—The chapel in the wilderness—A cocoa plantation—Cocoa trees and their fruit—Pounding the beans—A coffee plantation—Coffee berries—The ricefields—Threshing and winnowing—The Hermitage—The prophet's room—Man's necessities—A first night in the forest—Beetles, grasshoppers, locusts, cockroaches—Walking leaves—Praying prophets—Frogs—Owls—Parrots—Monkeys—Wild beasts and snakes—Thoughts and feelings—Rain—The tiger story—In the canoe—A walk in the forest—Horatio's dog—The bushmaster—The snake charmer—An adventure—The silk cotton tree—Strange superstitions—"No' me, de massa"—The return.

CONTENTS

XIV.

KIMBIA LAKES 212

A dangerous place—Pluck and courage—Dawn—Off in the boat—Our party—Weapons of defence—A lonely squatter—Points—In Kimbia Creek—Paddling—Leo—A labba——A monkey—Sambo—A Dutchman's bridge—Difficulties—The cutlass—A rest—Off again—The great savannah—The moca-moca—Kimbia Lake at last—Ita palms—A deathly silence—A picnic—Danger and difficulty—The drinking cup—Getting dark—Moonlight and shadows—In the river once more—Balmy sleep—Abarybanna.

XV.

AMONG THE ARAWAACK INDIANS . . . 228

Off once more—Wood-cutters—Sandhills—Maria Henrietta—Coomacka—A flotilla of canoes—The Indian chief—Wikky Creek—The Green Heart and other trees—The landing-place—Indian women and picknies—The Arawaacks—The Accawais—The Caribs—The Waraws—The Macoosis—General history—Their appearance—Description of the Caribs—Characteristics of the Waraws—Revenge of the Macoosis—The warlike Accawais—The subjects of our Mission—The good qualities of the Arawaacks—Their marriages—Marching to the settlement—Sight of a snake—Landmarks of the Arawaacks—Their instincts—The forest trees—The Indian's signals—The settlement—Calcuni—The Indian chapel and parson's benaab—No furniture—Service—Introduction to the families—How the days passed—Farewell!

LIST OF ILLUSTRATIONS.

A Coolie Lady		*Frontispiece*
An Orchid Associated with other Epiphytes	*Facing p.*	51
Mission House, N. A. Berbice	,, ,,	65
A Coolie Family	,, ,,	74
Selling Fish in Georgetown	,, ,,	74
Water Street, Georgetown	,, ,,	81
Cookie having a Gossip on the Way	,, ,,	82
Camp Street, Georgetown, showing Trench with Victoria Regia Lilies	,, ,,	88
Avenue of Palm Trees, Georgetown	,, ,,	90
A Chinese Wood-carrier	,, ,,	105
Cookie returning from Market	,, ,,	105
Strand, N. A. Berbice	,, ,,	107
An East Indian Beauty	,, ,,	113
Coolie House, Corentyne Coast, Berbice	,, ,,	115

LIST OF ILLUSTRATIONS

PARSON AND DEACONS	Facing p.	117
SLAVES LANDING FROM THE SHIP	,, ,,	156
"DE GREAT MASSA HAB MADE US FREE"	,, ,,	174
MATTED ROOTS OF COURIDA	,, ,,	187
INUNDATED FOREST	,, ,,	206
CREEK SCENE	,, ,,	216
CREEK, WITH TIGER'S BRIDGE	,, ,,	219
INDIAN BENAAB (ARAWAACKS)	,, ,,	228
INDIAN WOMAN, WITH HAMMOCK AND PEGALL	,, ,,	235
GROUP OF ACCAWAIS INDIANS	,, ,,	237
SECOND GROWTH FOREST	,, ,,	241
AN INDIAN SETTLEMENT	,, ,,	244

BRITISH GUIANA

I

OFF TO THE WEST INDIES AND THE SPANISH MAIN

"COME, tell us all about your travels," said my friend—"where you have been wandering during the last ten years. Tell us about the alligators, and the tigers, and the jaguars, and the bush-hogs, and the crab-dogs, and the monkeys, and the hard-backs, and all those other creatures that you have seen. And tell us about that strange and comparatively unknown land, where there are those vast savannahs which the foot of man has never trod, and those primeval forests where the sound of the white man's axe has never been heard, and those large rivers that go creeping lazily along to the sea, winding their way through the exuberance of tropical growth; and tell us about the black people, and the Chinese, and the coolies, and the aboriginal Indians in the interior. We must have it all, so compose yourself and begin."

It was a cold, bleak morning in November that the good ship *Incomparable* started out on her voyage of nearly five thousand miles. We were not many passengers, and so we soon became acquainted with each other. There was one person, however, whom we could not quite make out. He was neither an officer of the ship nor a passenger. And as he came down into the saloon regularly to dine with us we began to speculate as to who and what he might be. On inquiry we found that his work was a most important one. He had been sent on board to *adjust* the *compasses*.

Amongst all the wonderful contrivances of a modern steamship, there is none more essential to its safety and well-being than the compass. It is a little thing, but no ship could cross these seas without it. When neither sun nor stars are visible, and when the mariner is far out, thousands of miles from land, that little compass tells him in what direction to steer. It is the ship's guide when all other guides are lost. The winds may roar and blow a hurricane blast; the wild waves, lashed into fury, may roll mountains high, the ship may pitch and roll and plunge, and officers and men may quake, but the needle in the compass calmly and steadily points to the north. Without it the ancients hardly ever ventured to lose sight of land. With it, we can cross the trackless ocean and navigate the world. But how if the compass gets out of order? How if some of the delicate machinery connected with its working goes wrong? This does sometimes happen; hence the necessity for adjusting the compasses. As I sat on the deck looking out on the calm sea, with North Foreland in the distance and the lovely little town of Ramsgate with its "piers" and its people, I thought, "There are *Home compasses* that need adjusting. When things go wrong in the home, they go wrong everywhere. Discord there means discord all around. And how often a little thing disturbs the peace and harmony of years. As soon as you find cross-currents and contrary winds, take your bearings and look to your compass. Perhaps you may find that the Home compass is a little out. Conscience is not quite as susceptible as it used to be. A hardening process has been going on through contact with the world. The finger still points heavenward, but there have been disturbing influences. The magnetism of money, of some unworthy ambition, of some person or passion, has disturbed the magnetic needle, which always points towards God. Adjust your HOME *compasses*. There are *Political compasses*, too, that need adjusting, and *Ecclesiastical compasses* have OFTEN got wrong; but I must not dwell upon these, or our voyage will become interminably long. It was just growing dark as we passed Dover, and we could see the long row of lights quite plainly in the distance; a strong breeze had sprung up, and with it a heavy sea. In fact the wind blew half a gale, and as the old skipper looked out he said to me, "We are going to have a '*sneezer*' to-night." And a "*sneezer*" we had. As the night closed in upon us, wind and wave increased in fury, and the inky blackness of the night only added to our fears. The men went round seeing that all portholes were properly fastened and doors shut and barred, and passengers secured below, and lifebelts ready. And the battle between the floating ship and the wrathful sea began. The waves hissed and roared and leaped, coming down on the deck of the iron ship with the weight of a thousand tons, and with a crash like thunder; but the good ship, steadying herself for a moment beneath the shock, shook the waters savagely from her mane, and rising up on the incoming billow, rode triumphant o'er the waves. Thus through that dark night she fought the storm, and glad were we all when morning light dawned upon us.

A few days after this, as we were going down to dinner, the cry was heard "*A man overboard!*" Immediately a lifebelt was thrown out with a lighted fuse to it, for it was nearly dark, and orders were given to stop the ship. We could hear distinctly the cries of the man, "Help, ho!" A boat was lowered, and the first mate, with two seamen, pulled in the direction of the man; they just managed to grip him as he was going down exhausted and unconscious. Fastening a rope round his body, he was hauled on board and put into the hands of the doctor. It had been a severe shock to the poor man, and we saw nothing more of him during the whole of our voyage, he being sick and confined to his berth. Indeed, if he had not been a good swimmer, and in a fairly calm sea, he would have been lost. We did not fail to give the captain and the men our hearty congratulations and thanks for having so nobly snatched one from the jaws of death.

Thus far we had been hugging the shore, sailing along the south coast, for, as we learned, we had to call in at Dartmouth. Whilst the ship was "coaling," some of us went ashore, and a few pleasant hours were spent wandering about the quaint old town, admiring the hills and rambling on the banks of the beautiful river Dart.

At dusk the ship began to move slowly out of the harbour, and in a few minutes we were out on the great ocean. This time it was " Westward Ho." There was a fine sea on and a strong breeze. I stood on the deck, holding on to the ropes, watching the sun set on one side, and the receding shores of my native land on the other. A feeling of pensive sadness crept over me as I looked for the last time upon the darkening shadows of the hills: deepening, darkening—they are now but a dim outline; I rubbed my eyes—fading away. Thus all things go from us; this world itself will one day thus vanish, when we sail out on that larger ocean of eternity.

> " Adieu, adieu ! my native shore
> Fades o'er the waters blue ;
> The night winds sigh, the breakers roar
> And shrieks the wild seamew.
> Yon sun that sets upon the sea
> We follow in its flight ;
> Farewell awhile to him and thee
> My native land—Good-night."

Having fairly got out to sea, we began to look to our cabins, opening our trunks and bringing out what little things we had, to make ourselves comfortable. Some were already feeling bad, and praying that they might escape that sickness which, as the Irishman said, is a very "upsetting thing." One in my cabin seemed to be in the throes of an internal conflict. Something within said, "I want to come up"; whilst he replied, "You mustn't, just stop where you are." But the voice within, more determined than ever, said, "I will come up"; he as resolutely said, "You sha'n't." Thus the struggle went on; but, as I afterwards learned, the man had no peace until he had yielded, and set the prisoner free.

I thought it was rather cruel of one young fellow who came on deck to some young ladies who were trying bravely to hold up, but who were certainly very ill. "Well, young ladies," he said, "I see you are *enjoying* yourselves." They gave him such a look. He wasn't seen again for a day or two.

By eleven o'clock we had all crept into our holes, and were horizontally laid upon our respective shelves. But there was not much rest the first night. The thump of the engines and the thud of the screw, the jingling of glasses in the saloon and the crash of pots in the pantry, together with the rolling and pitching of the ship, all tend to keep you awake. Besides all this there is the difficulty of lying still. First you roll to one side, and then to the other. Now your feet are up, and you feel as if you were standing on your head—in another moment this position is reversed; then the ship gives a roll and a lurch, and if you don't grip the boards pretty tight you are pitched out of bed. One lady was thus thrown out, and her face was bruised as if she had been fighting; and a gentleman came bounding out over the side of his berth without any warning, breaking one or two glasses and damaging his arm.

Dinner-hour is, as a rule, one of the pleasantest hours on board ship; especially after the first day or two, when passengers have all found their sea-legs. It is at the dining-table that we put on our best looks, as well as our best apparel; the ladies in their charming dresses and the gentlemen in their evening suits. It is there that we get to know one another, and the luxury of conversation adds to the enjoyment of the repast. We had at our table a minister, a lawyer, a doctor, a sea captain, a stockbroker, and a merchant, besides other gentlemen and some ladies. And I was specially struck with the professional bias which tinged each man's outlook on men and things. If a subject came up for conversation, the legal aspect of it was pointed out sooner or later by the lawyer, and its influence on the Church or the moral life of the nation was dwelt on by the minister, and the doctor showed us how every physical fact bears directly or indirectly upon the different organs of the body, thus affecting the constitution of the individual, and through him the force and power of the whole community. The merchant, looking at the different things upon the table, was interested in finding out where they came from, what their original cost was, how much they would sell for, and what profit could be made out of them. Thus I saw how difficult it is for men to see things as they are. Indeed, we none of us do *that;* we only see things as they appear to us. And everything is more or less tinged by the medium through which we view it. The personal equation is often the most important part of a man's subject.

We had one character, however, amongst the gentlemen who afforded us no little amusement. He didn't seem to know much, but he was a great swell. He lived in Belgravia. At dinner he had two or three set phrases, which he uttered with the tone and gesture of an "Oracle." If any one made a more profound remark than usual, he would say, "I quite endorse the correctness of your remark." The rescuing of the man that fell overboard led to our talking one day about life — about its uncertainty, its brevity, its mystery.

"Life," said the doctor, "is *assimilation;* when the power to assimilate is gone, life is gone too. Or to put it in another way, it is the sum of the functions by which death is resisted."

"I quite endorse the correctness of your remark," cried out our "Oracle."

"*No*," said the minister. "Life is something more than assimilation; it is the undefinable entity of which assimilation is but a *modus operandi.*"

"Quite correct," chimed in the "Oracle."

"Life," said our legal representative, "has its laws; through those laws it works, and it will not work outside of them. Obedience to law is life. Lawlessness is death. Indeed, life and law are identical. My law is my life." This he said with a merry twinkle in his eye.

"I quite endorse the correctness of your remark," said Chesson, amid general laughter all round the table.

On the eighth day we sighted the Azores. Making for St. Michael's, one of the largest islands of this group, we entered the breakwater at Ponta Delgada. The view as we entered was charming. The white houses dotted along the hill-sides and the cultivated green fields, with here and there a little church, and the town lying at the base, formed a picture not to be forgotten. The climate here is warm and genial. Although it was well on into November, there were summer skies, balmy air and bright sunshine. We walked through the narrow streets of the old town, and then visited some of the large gardens, belonging to the Spanish and Portuguese gentry. There we saw orange trees, and grapes and apricots and green figs, and flowers in abundance. The one thing in the town that took our fancy was some beautiful vases and water goblets made of a specially fine red, silvery clay found in the interior. Specimens of these we bought and carried away with us, the price being very moderate.

Having taken in coals and cargo, we once more weighed anchor, and slowly steered for the open sea.

The night we left Ponta Delgada was one to be remembered. For the past week we had been sailing amid darkness and storm. But now, what a change! Inside that breakwater all was calm. The good ship, which had "walked the sea like a thing of life," was still. Her breathing was hushed; the ceaseless throb of her engines and the pulsations of her screw were no longer felt. A strange and bewitching stillness hovered around. Added to this was the beauty of the night. The moon so silent, yet so bright. The placid waters, like a mirror, reflecting both earth and sky. Right before us was the coast line, the little town, with its white houses, lying so peacefully at the foot of the hills. As the pale light of the moon shone upon the white buildings, and our ship began to move to the motions of wind and wave, we stood gazing wistfully; it was a picture never to be forgotten.

"How lovely!" I said to my fair companion.

"How sweetly peaceful!" she replied.

We got our deck-chairs, and under the stars we thought and talked of many things. There, rising out of the water to the east, is Orion.

"Do you see his arrows?"

"Yes; there they are."

Orion was a mighty hunter, and like most hunters, whether hunters after truth, after fame, after love, or after happiness, had difficulties and disappointments. In his wanderings he one day came to Chios, in the Ægean sea; there he saw Æro, the beautiful daughter of Œnopion. He no sooner saw her than he loved. Wondrous is the power of love, and strange as wonderful.

OFF TO THE WEST INDIES AND SPANISH MAIN

"Love rules the court, the camp, the grove;
Men below, and saints above;
For love is heaven, and heaven is love."

It took captive old Orion. We are its slaves still, and it is the only slavery that women, aye, and men too, prefer to freedom. As Shelley says—

"They who inspire it most are fortunate,
As I am now; but those who feel it most
Are happiest still."

Orion in love set to work. He cleared the island of wild beasts, and brought their skins as a present to his sweetheart. For her he toiled. To her he brought the products of his labour. The day at last, the nuptial day, was named. But the course of true love never did run smooth. The father of Æro was given to a policy of postponement. He *always* found some reason for putting off their marriage. Postponement and procrastination, both thieves of time, wore out Orion's patience. He could wait no longer. The fruit was ripe upon the tree. He would take the maiden by force. That was the fatal step. Better to have waited. The father and he entered into deadly conflict. Old Bacchus put out his eyes, and at last he was shot by an arrow that flew from the bow of Artemis, a virgin goddess that loved him passionately. After his death he was placed with his hound and his arrows among the stars, and one of the brightest constellations bears his name.

We looked at Orion as we sat there in our chairs, the night zephyrs of the sea playing around us, and right in a line with it towards the north was a beautiful bright star that followed us all the way. It was Capella, our star of hope and cheer. "Under what star do you live?" I said—

> "Is it the tender star of love?
> The star of love and dreams."

"There is no night," she said, "but that star can brighten, and no gloom but its rays can cheer. *I* will choose Venus. But under what star do *you* live?" she asked.

"Not Venus," I replied, "but Mars. I am born to conflict and resistance.

> "'The star of the unconquer'd will,
> He rises in my breast,
> Serene and resolute and still,
> And calm and self-possessed.'

"Have you ever noticed," said I, "how the hero and the loved one stand side by side in the world's battle?—*Venus* and *Mars*, so dissimilar yet so intertwined. Our great dramatist says of 'Desdemona,' 'She loved him for the dangers he had passed.' Thus MAN'S destiny and work are shown. HE struggles; SHE sustains. Man goes forth to the conflict, and returns wounded and weak. Love soothes his aching temples, heals his wounds, and restores his strength. As Milton says—

> "'For contemplation he, and valour formed
> For softness she, and sweet attractive grace;
> He for God only, she for God in him.'"

Thus we talked, and the hours flew fast as we sailed along, under the stars, in that tropical sea.

As we advance, at the rate of about three hundred knots a day, we find the temperature rising. A bright, blazing sun now shines overhead. The sky is blue and clear. The ocean is indeed a sea of glass. We have put off all our heavy clothing, and substituted for it the lightest of fabrics. Still it is too hot. I shall not soon forget my first experience of a real tropical sun and a sultry tropical day. There was not a breath of wind stirring. Even the motion of the ship did not create any breeze. The sea was a dead calm. As we sat, the perspiration oozed out of us. We seemed to be entering into the mouth of a hot oven. People's faces began to assume the most extraordinary colours. "It IS hot," was the general salutation. One gentleman, who was rather stout, mopping up the perspiration as it rolled like brooklets down his face, said "This is my twelfth handkerchief this morning," and it was only half-past eleven then.

"You are *in liquidation*," I said.

"Yes; and there will not be much of me left, I fear, when I have done."

It is hot on deck, hotter in the saloon, and hottest in the cabins. Oh those ship cabins in the tropics! and especially if, as sometimes happens, your porthole has to be closed on account of the seas. The hot-room in a Turkish bath is a fool to it. You lie down at night, your face becomes livid, you gasp for breath; in five minutes you are in a beautiful and copious perspiration—a sensation of "melting away" steals over you, and you give yourself up to languor, which ends in a state of unconscious collapse. Not a few creep out in pyjamas or dressing-gown, under cover of night, and sleep on deck. There, with your pipe, and in your easy chair, you can look up at the stars, and think of many things, till—

"Tired nature's sweet restorer, balmy sleep,"

OFF TO THE WEST INDIES AND SPANISH MAIN

closes your eyes, and leads you into the land of dreams.

There were many interesting things that we passed at sea. In the earlier part of our voyage we were called up to see a huge whale, some little distance on our starboard side, moving in the same direction as the ship, but not going so fast. The captain said it appeared to be about sixty feet long; the back of the whale was plainly visible above the surface of the sea, and every now and then it would lift its head and send a spurt of water right up into the air.

The shoals of porpoise that appeared gamboling at our ship's side afforded us some little amusement. They came just as the storm subsided and as we neared the Azores. There seemed to be hundreds of them—coming up out of the depths, swimming along by our side, then turning a somersault in the water, and again lost to our view. But it was not till we got into tropical waters that we had our first sight and taste of "flying-fish." There are many people whose faith will not allow them to accept these stories about "fish flying." They can believe that a whale swallowed Jonah, or, if necessary, that Jonah swallowed the whale; but "flying-fish" is too much for their credulity. It is said that in "ye olden time" a sailor-boy came home after a long voyage and told his mother about fish flying like birds. The old lady shook her head and said, "John, John, what a liar you are. You think me believe you?" But when he told her about fishing in the Red Sea, and at the first throw of the net hauling up a chariot-wheel made all of gold and inlaid with diamonds, which he supposed was one of the wheels of Pharaoh's chariot which came off whilst he was pursuing the Israelites—"Lord, bless us!" she said; "now that *is* possible. Tell me such stories as *that*, and I'll believe you; but never tell me of such things as 'flying-fish.'"

Such fish, however, are a scientific certainty. On several mornings we saw them rising up out of the sea, and flying like a bevy of birds, not a few of them alighting on the deck of our ship, which were soon picked up by the sailors and handed over to our cook. They were very nice eating, and we considered ourselves fortunate in having what few get, viz., "flying-fish," for our breakfast. A learned friend of mine tells me that more than thirty species of these flying-fish are known. They swim in shoals of from one dozen to a hundred or more. To any one watching they spring up out of the sea all at once, darting in the same direction through the air. They rise to a height of thirty or

OFF TO THE WEST INDIES AND SPANISH MAIN

forty feet, flying a distance of two hundred yards or more, and then alight in the water again. If fish can fly, why can't we. Give us the wings and we'll try.

But we are now within sight of Barbadoes, or Little Britain, as the natives love to call it. And truly a pleasant sight it is to look upon the rising headlands and hills as they stand out against the sky. Soon we shall be in Carlisle Bay. Already we see a number of vessels riding at anchor—some discharging and others taking in cargo. But it is only as we begin to let go the anchor that we note the peculiarities of the people and place. At once we are surrounded by a flotilla of picturesque little boats. Each boat has one or two pullers besides the captain. They are mostly black or coloured people. Their object is to engage your attention and get you to hire their boat. At once the business begins. Each man calls out to you to remember *Mary Ann*, or the beautiful boat *Lilly*. "No," says another, "massa want de *Pearl; Pearl* de boat for massa." "I knows you," says a third. "You remember *Jane*, de beautiful *Jane!* *Jane* take you ober in no time; she sail like a duck. All right, sir, de lubly *Jane* am your boat—Number 63. Don't forget, sir—Number 63." And so twenty or thirty are shouting at you all at once, till you are utterly confused, and this they keep up for hours. Then there are the divers. They have a little box, shaped nearly like a coffin, only not quite so big. " A bitt, sir ; a sixpence, sir." Throw it over, and the smallest silver coin thrown into the sea, they will not fail to find it and fetch it up. For a shilling or less they will dive down and swim right under the ship, coming out on the other side. For hours, after the ship has anchored, passengers are kept alive with these noisy and persevering people.

When you first step ashore at Bridgetown you begin to realise that you have at last entered into a tropical city. The white and dusty streets, the blazing sun overhead, the black and coloured faces, the wooden houses with their jalousies and verandahs, the mules and asses, the little carts with their peculiar vegetable produce—all these indicate that you have at last entered into a new world. We strolled down the main street at Bridgetown, called at the post-office and the icehouse, went on to view Nelson's monument and Trafalgar Square ; thence by car to Hastings, and on from thence a little way into the country. The heat was oppressive, and the Badians themselves irrepressible. One black man followed us all about

—would be our "guide, counsellor, and friend"—until we called in the aid of the police, when he decamped and left us alone. We bought a few curios and some different kinds of fruit peculiar to the tropics, and refreshed ourselves with "ice-cream" and "cocktails" and lemon squash, and then made our way back to the ship. By 6.15 p.m. we weighed anchor, and once more began to plough our way through the darkness and the deep, making straight for the South American coast.

II

GUIANA, OR THE WILD COAST

HOW welcome is the first faint outline of "land ahead" to those who have been for weeks tossed upon the briny deep. It is like the sight of water to the thirsty traveller, or like the first glimpse of the old house at home after years of wandering. As soon as the news spread that land could be seen we all crowded on deck. Even ladies who had been too ill to come up out of their cabins now got courage to creep out, and we were astonished to see faces that we had hardly ever seen before. "There is the land, sir!" "Where?" said my friend. "Don't you see the big mountains?" said the lawyer, with a merry twinkle in his eye. Alas! there are no mountains to be seen on reaching this tropical land. The mountains are in the interior, but the coast lands are low-lying and flat. Owing to this flatness, the first view we

GUIANA, OR THE WILD COAST

get of land from the deck of the ship is a long, irregular line of thick bush, with groups of elevated trees, these being chiefly palm trees—the cocoanut palm, or the long, straight cabbage palm; and here and there a tall chimney is to be seen, indicating the proximity of a sugar plantation. All along the coast is skirted by mud flats and sandbanks, and the approach to the rivers needs careful and skilful pilotage. As we have to enter the mouth of the Demerara river, on which the chief city, the city of Georgetown, stands, we will sit down quietly, and I will give you some little account of the Wild Coast whilst the ship slowly ploughs her way to the stelling.

Going into a school one day in England, I asked a number of children, "Where is British Guiana?" "On the map of the world, sir," shouted one little fellow. Well, so it is, and it has been there for several hundred years, and yet very few know anything about it. The best things, as a rule, take a good deal of finding out—

> "The jewel that we find, we stoop and take it
> Because we see it; but what we do not see
> We tread upon and never think of it."

Guiana, *Guyana*, or *Guayana* was so named, say some, from a tribe of aborigines or Indians called "*Guyannols.*" The Dutch, adopting the word "Guiana" into their vocabulary, gave it the meaning of "Wild Coast" or "Wild Place." Who really discovered it is uncertain. Some say Columbus in 1498, others say Vasco Menes and Diego de Ordas; but we must leave that point to be settled by the critics. One thing we know, and that is that Sir Walter Raleigh visited it in 1595, and Lawrence Keymis, one of Raleigh's captains, in 1596 and 1597. So that we English have a kind of historic interest in the place; indeed, we have claims upon Guiana dating back three hundred years.

Guiana, or the Wild Coast, is in some respects a strange and wonderful country. There has been a halo of romance about it since the days of Sir W. Raleigh, "the gallantest knight that ever was." In 1595, just over three hundred years ago, he sailed up the Orinoco, and marched into the interior in search of that fascinating place called *El Dorado*, the *golden* or *gilded land*. According to the descriptions of those days, "The gold coloured capital of El Dorado was built upon a vast lake, surrounded by mountains, so impregnated with the precious metals that they shone with a dazzling splendour." Disappointed in his undertakings, he returned home, and because he did not find this golden land the gallant hero—lost his head.

Whether an El Dorado of this kind exists on this side the Atlantic we cannot tell, but the gold which Raleigh sought in vain is being found now, and the diamonds with which he intended to enrich his monarch's crown are only being picked up to-day, three hundred years after. "One merchant quite recently received forty-two diamonds from one of his placers in the interior. Twelve of these were submitted to Professor Harrison for analysis, and were declared to be genuine diamonds." But this is only the beginning. It is but within the past few years that the auriferous regions of British Guiana have been made to yield up their precious treasures. Since 1884 prospecting has gone on vigorously, and numerous companies have been formed. Large numbers of gold diggers have been sent into the interior, with what results the following extracts from the Blue Book will show. The districts from which the largest quantities of gold have as yet been taken are the Essequebo and its tributaries. From the " Puruni, and Potaro, the Barima and Barama rivers in the north - west district, good results have been obtained. Rich deposits have been found on

BRITISH GUIANA

the right bank of the river Potaro, and this part of the colony has given better results for its area than any other." (See "B. G. Directory," p. 12.) Since 1884 the annual shipment of gold has steadily increased. Here are the official returns:—

	Ounces.	Value.
1884	250	£1,019
1885	939	3,249
1886	6,518	23,342
1887	11,906	44,427
1888	14,570	64,403
1889	28,282	109,234
1890	62,615	234,324
1891	101,298	375,289
1892	133,146	492,937
1893	137,629	510,710
1894	134,047	496,899

making a grand total of 631,200 ounces of gold exported from the colony during these eleven years, valued at £2,355,833.

"Guyana," or the Wild Coast, applies to all that land on the north-east of South America which lies between 3° 30' and 8° 40' north latitude and between 50° and 60° west longitude. If you look at your map you will find that the coast line is bounded on the south by that king of rivers the Amazon. This river winds its way through tropical forest and savannah for more than 2,000 miles. The main trunk of this enormous stream, which for length of course and volume of water has no parallel, drains an area of about 2,000,000 square miles, and then rolls into the Atlantic with an estuary 150 miles wide. On the north, Guiana is bounded by the Orinoco, another mighty stream. This is the third largest river of South America. This river has about fifty mouths, and it needs them all to pour out its vast volume of water. Seven of these mouths are navigable by large vessels, but the chief mouth, which is called "The Serpent's Mouth," is eighteen miles broad. The direct course of the Orinoco does not exceed 1,200 miles, but take its extraordinary windings into account, and its course would be over 2,000 miles. It drains a surface of 400,000 square miles. These are the two outstretched arms of Guiana, bounding it on the north and on the south; in fact, with the Atlantic Ocean, they almost encircle it. For it is a curious geographical fact that these two large rivers, so far apart, communicate with each other. A person setting out on a circular tour might sail out of the Atlantic into the Amazon, out of the Amazon into the Rio Negro, out of the Rio Negro into the Cassiquiari, out of the Cassiquiari into the Orinoco, down the Orinoco and into the Atlantic again, having thus sailed all round this immense tract of country called Guiana. But this larger Guiana is divided politically into five parts, viz., Venezuelan or Spanish, British, Dutch, French, and Brazilian or Portuguese. The boundaries of some of these have not yet been definitely fixed.

The part in which we are interested is British Guiana. It lies between the 1st and 9th degree of north latitude and the 57th and 61st degree of west longitude. It is about twice the size of England and Wales, having an area of about 100,000 square miles. The Dutch seem to have been the first to attempt colonisation here. So far back as 1580, a number of Dutch traders effected a settlement on the banks of the "Pomeroon."

In 1613, under the leadership of Joost van der Hooge, a settlement was formed on a small island at the mouths of the Cuyuni and the Massuruni, where they found the remains of a fort, which they repaired. This fort was afterwards known as "Kyk-over-al" ("look" or "see over all").

In 1621 the Dutch West India Company was formed, and they had given to them ex-

GUIANA, OR THE WILD COAST

clusive control over all their settlements on the "Wild Coast." They also undertook to supply their colonists with negro slaves from Africa. This was the beginning of that great curse, negro slavery, in British Guiana. The sugar and coffee estates were to be worked by these kidnapped and enslaved Africans.

> " I would not have a slave to till my ground,
> To carry me, to fan me while I sleep,
> And tremble while I wake, for all the wealth
> That sinews bought and sold have ever earned."
> —COWPER'S "Task," B. ii.

In 1624 Abraham Van Peere formed a settlement on the river Berbice. Here the colonists seemed to thrive, for a hundred years after this, Berbice colony was granted a Constitution by the States General of Holland. This was in 1732. In 1781 the British took possession of the whole Dutch West Indian colonies, but at the peace of 1783 they were again restored. They were then taken possession of by the French, who built forts on both sides of the river Demerara at its mouth. In 1796 the colonies of Demerara, Essequebo, and Berbice were again in possession of the Dutch, and in 1803 they were finally surrendered to the British, in whose possession they have ever since remained and

BRITISH GUIANA

progressed, being formally ceded to us by treaty in 1814.

British Guiana is divided into three provinces, viz., Berbice, Demerara, and Essequebo. Through these provinces flow three great rivers. The river Berbice, which discharges itself into the Atlantic about 57 miles to the east of the Demerara. It is about two miles and a quarter broad at its mouth. Its source is as yet unexplored. Vessels of 12 feet draft can ascend this splendid water-way for about 105 miles, and of 7 feet draft 180 miles. The influence of the tide is felt nearly up to that point. It abounds with fish of nearly all sizes and kinds. This river has many tributaries or creeks. In its course it is very tortuous, and away up towards its source it forms the Christmas cataract and the Itabou cataract. Forty-five miles to the east, as it passes along, is drained by this river and its tributaries, and forty-five miles to the west. So that it drains an area of about 18,000 miles.

The Demerara river, on which the capital city stands, was called by Raleigh and his followers Lemdrāre, by the Spaniards Rio-de-Mirara (*i.e.*, The Wonderful River), and by the Dutch Innemāry, or Demerary. The source of this river is known to the Indians alone. Its current is very powerful, especially towards its mouth, where it is about two miles wide. It is said to flow at the rate of seven or eight knots an hour, and the under-currents are equally powerful, and act much in the manner of whirlpools. It is notorious that few persons who have the misfortune to fall into it are ever saved. Whether they are borne away by the strong under-current, or sucked in by the eddying wave, or devoured by the greedy sharks, which in hundreds swarm about at its mouth, it is difficult to say. The colour of its water is of a dirty yellow, made so by the clayey soil or mud, which is washed down by its rapid waters and deposited at its mouth in banks or mud flats, thus forming natural barriers at the entrance of the stream to any very large vessels. It is navigable for fair-sized ships about ninety miles.

The Essequebo is the largest river in British Guiana; hence it has been called the younger brother of the Orinoco. It is 620 miles long, and twenty miles wide at its mouth. At its mouth are situated several islands, some of which are from twelve to fifteen miles long. The principal islands are Leguan (from El Guano), which has several sugar estates in it, and Wakenaam, signifying "in want of a name," which also is populated and engaged in making that same sweet commodity. I had the pleasure of travelling with two Scotch ministers, one of whom had been the minister on that island, and the other was going there to take up his appointment.

The Essequebo has many large tributaries. There is the Cuyuni river, which flows into it from the south-west about 70 miles from the sea. The course of this river is through a large valley bounded on every side by mountains except to the east, extending 280 miles in length, and expanding from 70 miles to 150 miles in breadth. All the waters of this extensive valley discharge themselves into the Cuyuni, which may be denominated its chief trunk or grand drainer. And it discharges itself into the Essequebo. Then there is the Rupununi, the Potaro, the Massuruni, on which Her Majesty's penal settlement stands. The Potaro or Black River is famous for its "Kaieteur Falls," which are likely to outrival the famous Niagara. The head of this fall is 1,130 feet above the level of the sea. The breadth of the river is from 250 feet to 350 feet according to the season; the average depth is 20 feet, and this mass of water dashes over a precipice 900 feet high with a noise like thunder. The grandeur and magnitude of this fall transcends description.

GUIANA, OR THE WILD COAST

But we must come back to our provinces. From what has already been said, you will see that much of this land is *terra incognita*. It is a new world, of which the old world knows very little. It is only along a narrow strip of seacoast that people live. The interior still forms the happy hunting-ground. About 130 square miles out of 100,000 square miles has been put under cultivation. We talk about population increasing so fast that it will overtake the means of subsistence. Would that Malthus could have opened his eyes on these far-stretching savannahs and these interminable forests. What is wanted is not land, but people to till it. Here we have a mine of wealth in forest and river, and plane and savannah; but none, or very few, to draw it out and utilise it. When we leave our coast lands and strike into the interior, we come to our sandhills and our far-stretching savannahs, our mountains and immense forests, all lying in a state of nature, the dwelling-place of wild animals and Indian tribes. The command of God to man is to replenish the earth and subdue it. Our work lies before us; willing hearts and active hands are what is wanted. That British Guiana has vast resources cannot be questioned, but these resources are only imperfectly known, and to a few. Up the rivers and in the interior we are brought into contact with large fertile valleys, capable of supporting thousands upon thousands of cattle, vast forests, rich in every kind of wood, and immense undulating savannahs, all waiting to be opened up and utilised. A grand, almost inexhaustible field for capital and industry is thus opened to our view.

The wealth of a country is to be found originally in its land. There can be no question about the richness and productiveness of the soil of British Guiana. As Dalton says, "It is an alluvial soil which has not its equal in the world, save perhaps the overflooded plains of the Nile." So prolific are the plants and so luxuriant their growth, that to ensure an abundance of fruit it seems only necessary to commit seeds and shoots to the earth, and cut out from time to time the greater part of the wood of the trees. The great difficulty of the gardener and farmer here, is not too little exuberance, but too much. The wealth of tropical growth often disheartens and overwhelms men. Leave a field uncultivated for a short time and it is overrun with "bush." Leave the bush alone and it becomes a forest. Leave the forest alone and it becomes a jungle, a tangled mass of trees, of shrubs, of grasses, of creeping parasites, of twisted lianos, and the lurking place of stinging insect, hissing reptile, and devouring beast. But it is said, " Is not the rich soil confined to the coast lands now under cultivation?" By no means. The old planters found the richest soil higher up the rivers. Men who have lived in the interior assure us "that these interior lands will produce far more sugar, coffee, cocoa, rice, than the sea coast, and that with half the labour." In addition to this, the interior lands are far more healthy. Of course I do not mean every part, but I refer chiefly to the higher lands, the plains and forests above the sandhills, and the elevated and undulating savannahs. Of these latter we have a large number. One writer estimates that of the 100,000 square miles which this land contains, 35,000 is of open, flat, undulating savannah. There are 5,000 miles of grass-covered mountains, and 60,000 miles of dense forests which even in the daytime are almost as dark as night.

Savannah is from the Spanish word "Sābāna," and means a great plain or prairie. Sabana, which is the word for "bed-sheet," denotes a great tract of land, spread out and more or less level—a kind of limitless meadow. What an ocean is in the aqueous realm, a savannah is in the terrene realm. It is a vast expanse of land, stretching far away beyond the limit of unaided vision, often bounded only by the horizon line. Of course these savannahs are not all alike; some are great swampy places, especially in the rainy season, swampy simply because there has been as yet no outlet made for their waters. In these swamps tall, rank grasses grow, often to the height of six or eight feet; you cannot see over them. In these grasses are all kinds of reptiles, serpents, lizards, tortoises, and insects that prick and bite and sting, and sometimes of devouring beasts. Then there are others that are fine, undulating grassy plains, well suited for pasturage and even for other forms of agriculture. Sir R. Schomburg, speaking of these savannahs, says, "They appeared to me to resemble the 'Darling' downs of Queensland, as the grass not only holds supremacy over the flat lands, but passes over hill and mountain extirpating the trees and bushes, as though the hand of man with axe, compass, and line had directed the demarcation so beautifully defined." The surface of these savannahs is seldom flat for any considerable distance. "It would be difficult," says the great traveller, "to find a level of a mile in length. It is all 'ups' and 'downs,' elevations and depressions, from five feet to sixty." It is very interesting to read about that great savannah on which "Pirari" is situated, a village occupied by "Macusi" Indians. It is supposed to cover a space of 14,400 square miles. This, it is thought, was once the bed of an inland lake. By one of those upheavals which are not unknown in new countries, Nature burst its barriers, and thus found a passage for its waters into the Atlantic. This theory explains the ancient tradition of an "inland sea," and the city of the gold-besprinkled Manoa which fired the ardour of Sir W. Raleigh and the Spanish adventurers. It is none other than the site of the once famous El Dorado. Here is Schomburg's description :

"On leaving the river Rupununi we passed over undulating ground, thinly covered with shrubs of stunted appearance, and bright yellow or pink flowers. We turned round a small hillock, and before us was one of those small groves of Mauritia palms which give to the savannahs of South America so characteristic an appearance. This graceful tree, with its fan-shaped leaves, alone afforded the scanty shade to be found in those arid plains, while it contributed to the picturesque scene before us. The different tints of the savannah which extended to the Pacaraima mountains might have been compared to a sea of verdure, which illusion was powerfully increased by the waving motion of the deceptive mirage. Isolated groups of trees rose like islands from the bosom of this sea ; and a few scattered palms, with their tall trunks appearing like masts in the horizon, assisted in conveying to our imagination the seducing picture of the 'Leguna de Parima' or the Inland Sea, with its hundreds of canoes floating on its bosom."

Some of the finest savannahs are said to be those on the Berbice river, and lying between the Berbice and the Corentyne. The Ituni downs are a splendid example. Rowing up the Berbice river with the Indians, we struck into the forest. After about two hours' brisk walking, during which we ascended sandhills covered with trees, we emerged on to the open plain. The view that burst upon our sight was splendid. Far as the eye could see was the grass-covered plain, here and there were clumps of trees, chiefly the Ita palm, and down on our left could be distinctly traced the water valley of the Ituni. Beyond that was again to be seen the dark border-line of the forest. Away to the north could be seen lying down what appeared to us "deer" or wild cattle.

These savannahs on the westward side extend a distance of about forty-five miles, and on the eastward as far as the sea-coast. Cattle farming is carried on pretty extensively up the Corentyne coast, *i.e.*, the East Coast. Sometimes the cattle stray inland, and become wild. Some of them become the prey of tigers and jaguars. Horses that have grown wild are there too. Going home one year for six months, we determined to give our horse a rest, and so he was sent into the savannah. Away he wandered, close up to the Corentyne river. Men were sent after him on our return, and they found him kicking up his heels and snorting with the wild ones. Throwing the lasso, they caught him, and only in time, for the tigers were coming amongst them. A number of skeletons were lying about, and one horse, with its throat all torn, was killed the night before.

Of the climate, much has been written, and more has been said. In England it is considered to be little better than the West Coast of Africa, which has been called the White Man's Grave. Trollope said, "There never was a land so ill-spoken of, and never one that deserved it so little." And he said this after visiting it. He called it "the Elysium of the tropics," "the West Indian happy valley"—the one true and actual Utopia of the Carribean Seas—"the Transatlantic Eden." We do not ask you to adopt Trollope's opinion. Truth is generally found in the middle. Between the "White Man's Grave" and the "Transatlantic Eden" the truth about the climate is to be found. Many Europeans who have lived here to a good old age consider it delightful. For one thing, we are not exposed to those sudden changes of temperature which are so trying to weak and even strong constitutions. There is a uniformity of temperature all the year round. It varies from 74° in the morning to 84° in the shade at noon. Indeed, it is one of the steadiest climates in the world. We have no November fogs and no December chilling blasts. Frost and snow are absolutely unknown. The natives here have no idea of what a snowstorm means. Then, again, we are favoured with a steady breeze from the sea nearly all the year round. British Guiana lies in the main track of the equinoctial currents, and so from January to December we have a steady, cool breeze. In our hottest months, and in the rainy seasons, there is sometimes an intermission, and then we all cry out.

For some complaints, and especially those affecting the lungs and chest, this is a splendid climate. Pulmonary consumption is a thing almost unknown. "Tubercular phthisis," says one doctor, "I have never met with here." Some who could not possibly live in England on account of chest complaints, can live and enjoy life in this country. "If physicians at home," says one medical man, "knew of the advantages offered by this climate, they would oftener send their consumptive patients to this genial clime." Of course we have our diseases and death. These are not always attributable to the climate when they are said to be. With care, if a man's constitution be sound, a man may live here as long as anywhere. In the interior parts of the colony the purity of the air is proverbial, and especially in the dry season. At night the stars appear like brilliants in the deep azure sky, and even in the daytime planets can be sometimes seen. In the lowlands and the swampy places we get the miasma and the fever, but the highlands and the forests are never found to be unhealthy to Europeans. Live wisely and you will live well, and in all probability your days will be long in the land.

III

THE LAND WHERE SUGAR GROWS

HAVING told you something about the Wild Country, I must now tell you about that portion of it which is inhabited, and where the sugar grows. Who has not heard of Demerara? What difference of opinion there is about it! One calls it the "Transatlantic Eden," another "The Devil's Mud Flat." One having been, and gone away, thanks God that he has got out of it, and hopes never to put his head into it again. Another sings in joyous strain—

> "I have been there, and still would go;
> 'Tis like a little heaven below."

Mr. Bronkhurst, in his very interesting volume, says the following lines were found in an old escritoire which once belonged to a learned member of the Civil Service—

THE LAND WHERE SUGAR GROWS

"Demerara, land of trenches,
Giving out most awful stenches ;
Land of every biting beast
Making human flesh its feast ;
Land of swizzles, land of gin,
Land of every kind of sin !
Why have I been doomed to roam
Far, so far, away from home?"

Whatever kind of a place it is, it has already earned for itself the title of " The Magnificent Province." It is not quite *the* jewel in the British Crown, but it is one of them. Demerara is not the Wild Country, but it is *in* the Wild Country. It is that part which has been reclaimed and subdued. It is what we may call the hem of Guiana's garment, the borderland of this tropical "Canaan"; and while there are those who have brought up an evil report of the land which they have searched, there are others, like Caleb, who say, "It is a land flowing with milk and honey ; let us go up at once and possess it, for we are well able" (Numb. xiii. 30).

One thing about this land we must say, and that is, it is a *warm* one. Any one coming here is sure of a warm welcome. I looked at my thermometer this morning at half-past twelve o'clock, in the house, and of course in the shade, and it registered 94°. Out in the sun I have seen it 120°. The mean annual temperature is 84°.

We have only two seasons in the year, what my friend calls "*the roasting season*," which is the dry one, and during which you can be "*underdone*" or "*overdone*," according to your taste; and the "*broiling season*," which is the wet one, during which we have "*grave*," not to say "*gravy*," smells. The latter season has just set in, and the rain comes down in such torrents and with such persistence as to make you think a second deluge is no longer impossible. As the old sailors used to say, it only leaves off raining to commence *pouring*. During this season all the animals creep into the ark. The weather here is not so *feminine* as it is in England; that is, it is not so given to change. You can depend upon it. When it means to rain, it *does* rain, and when it means to be dry, it is dry—and everybody else too. It is the dry season that is the hottest. A stone statue would not feel cold then. From the end of July till the middle of December we have nothing but bright sunshine, and lovely moonlight nights in between. And the moonlight out here surpasses description. So light is it sometimes, that you could see to read the newspaper outside. There is a softness and a charm about it that makes it look like a fairy scene. On such a night, with all the rich luxuriance of tropical trees around, you seem to be standing in Fairyland. Many a time have I stood out in the garden entranced. Up above is the moon.

> "Through the fleecy clouds she sails along,
> Arrayed in silvery brightness."

All the trees are as still as icicles, and quite as sparkling; they seem to be under some magic spell—not a leaf stirs, and they glisten with a kind of glinted, frosted hue. You look around—it is as light as day, only it is a peculiar soft and soothing light. In that light you can see many things, for it makes fairy phantoms real, and real things fairy phantoms. A man that has once been in the tropics will never say that "the moon is made of green cheese." If he does, it will be a sure proof that he has been moonstruck, and is *luna-tic*. I used to wonder at the people, when I came here at first, saying, as I went to the door on a moonlight night without my hat, "Parson, you going get moonstruck; bettah cover you head." "All right," I would say, and at once covered my head. If a man falls asleep outside with his face exposed to the rays of the moon, in all probability he will wake up with his face swollen and drawn on one side, like a person that has had a stroke. I have seen such cases. An old writer says, "In the lowlands of tropical countries no attentive observer of nature will fail to witness the power exercised by the moon over the seasons, and also over animal and vegetable nature. As regards the latter, it may be stated that there are certainly thirteen springs and thirteen autumns in Demerara in the year; for so many times does the sap of trees ascend to the branches and descend to the roots. For example, 'wallaba,' a tree somewhat resembling mahogany, if cut down in the dark, a few days before the *new moon*, is one of the most durable woods in the world for house-building, posts, &c.; in that state attempt to split it, and with the utmost difficulty it will be riven in the most jagged and unequal manner. Cut down another wallaba, that grew within a few yards of the former, at *full moon*, and the tree can be easily split into the finest smooth shingles, of any desired thickness, or into staves for making casks; but in this state applied to house-building purposes it speedily decays. Bamboos if cut at the dark moon will endure for ten or twelve years; if at full moon, they will be rotten in two or three.

THE LAND WHERE SUGAR GROWS

Thus it is with most, if not all the forest trees." (R. M. Martin, F.S.S.)

The same writer observes, " I have seen in Africa the newly littered young perish in a few hours at the mother's side, if exposed to the rays of the full moon. Fish becomes rapidly putrid, and meat, if left exposed, incurable or unpreservable by salt. The mariner heedlessly sleeping on deck, becomes afflicted with nyctalopia, or night blindness; at times the face is hideously swollen; the maniac's paroxysms are renewed with fearful vigour at the full moon and the change." Do we not call those who suffer from mental diseases, or who are out of their mind, lunatics? *Luna* is the Latin for moon, and this very name implies that the moon has some occult influence over their mental condition. The power of Queen Luna is only partially known. In the tidal movements of the vast ocean we see something of it, but in those smaller tidal waves that pertain to the atmosphere, the clouds, the rivers, the sap and circulation of trees and plants, and even the vital forces of animals and men, we know very little. One thing, however, we know, and that is that this is a land of "enchanting moonshine."

The land where sugar grows is a land of equality. Not equality amongst the people; for in that respect we have the most glaring inequalities. Here the planter has long been the lord of the soil, if not the lord of creation. He has made our laws, and to a large extent administered them. And he has always had an eye to his own interest. In fact, he considers he has made the colony, *ergo* the colony ought to exist for him. He is the universal sweetener. But for him we should have "no cakes and ale." He is the one-eyed man in the kingdom of the blind.

The equality we have here is in the land rather than in the people. For instance, our days and nights are equal all the year round. At a quarter to six every morning the sun shines through your window, at a quarter past six every night he sinks down behind the western horizon. It is just the same in January as in June.

Then we have an equality in temperature. All the year round the thermometer registers about the same. It never drops down to freezing point and then runs up to summer heat. You don't require a change of underclothing on account of the change in temperature. You can wear the same light flannels in December as you wear in August.

The equality in temperature gives us a sameness in the vegetative aspects of nature. Trees are always green, flowers are always blooming, fruits are always ripe. We never see bare hedges, or leafless trees, or gardens without a sign of vegetation, such as may be seen in the winter time at home. Here the birds are always singing, and the gardens are always full of bloom. It is a summer that knows no winter except that which man creates, namely, " the winter of our discontent."

But this land is not only a land of equality; it is also a very *sweet land*. One other thing I have noticed in this land is, that it produces a large number of sweet things. It is a very sweet land. Thousands of acres around us here produce nothing but large sticks of sweet cane. These, when properly squeezed, give us 150,000 hogsheads of sugar and upwards. What a large cup of tea all that sugar would sweeten! And then think of the thousands of puncheons of "golden syrup," all brought out of the land. And it would give us a lot more if we would only bestow a little more labour upon it. Why, even our potatoes here are "sweet potatoes," and our cassava is "sweet cassava," and the plantains, when kept a little become "sweet plantains." In fact, what is called the saccharine element is found in large proportions in nearly all our vegetables and fruits. It is a "sweet country," and they ought to be sweet and pleasant people who live in it—and many of them are. Things that are not sweet when grown in England, become sweet when planted here. Would it not be a grand thing if we could take all the men and women with soured dispositions and plant them in this land till they became *sweetened*. I wonder, is it the soil or the sun that puts this sweetness into things, or is it the nature of the plant to select only those elements that are saccharine? It is probably the latter. Let us, like the sugarcane, select from the world around us those elements which will develop a sweet disposition and a noble spirit. A little more sunshine in the lives of those who have been embittered, and especially that soul sunshine which emanates from Him who is called the " Sun of Righteousness," and they would become sweeter, cheerier, and better. Love is the great sweetener of life, and " *God is Love.*"

Another characteristic of this land is its exuberant vitality. Everything seems to be alive—the air you breathe, the ground you tread upon, the water you drink. You cannot walk out in the garden without your feet and ankles being covered with " bête-rouge." This is a very small insect that you can hardly see with the naked eye; they make their way through your stockings and produce a most

[*To face p.* 51.

AN ORCHID ASSOCIATED WITH OTHER EPIPHYTES.

painful irritation. The ladies when they come in, and even gentlemen too, must at once retire to the bath, and try what soap and water will do to rid them of these torments. If you avoid the grass and keep to the road, then you have, if it be night, the frogs jumping from under your feet; and at certain seasons the air is filled with millions of sandflies (*Similium pertinax*). These come against your face and neck, and you feel as if a thousand needle-points were pricking into you at the same time. These sandflies are so minute that you cannot see them, but you are soon made aware of their presence. Mosquitoes are bad, but sandflies are worse. Plucking a beautiful flower, I was just lifting it up to my nose to draw in its perfume, when a friend by my side said "Don't." "Why?" I asked. "Because in many flowers there are small insects lodging, and you might draw them up into your nostrils and suffer very much in consequence."

The richness of the soil here and the profusion of plant life are well known. Tropical growth and tropical exuberance characterise field and forest. Land that has once been cultivated if left alone soon becomes a tangled mass of vegetation, difficult for a man to pass through. Creeping plants and floral vines spring up and entwine themselves around the larger trees and hang in festoons from the branches, sometimes making a very plain tree one mass of floral beauty. Nature here seems to gambol and delight in her prodigality. Hanging up in my drawing-room is what is called "the leaf of life"—*Byrophyllum calycinum.* It is so called because every part of it is so full of life that, put it where you will, it "sprouts," and develops both roots and buds. Hang it up to a gas-pipe and it will keep green and fresh for months; if there is the least moisture it will grow and propagate. Put the leaves of this plant on moist soil, and they will begin to grow and form a quantity of plants on each leaf. It would seem almost to be a "leaf" of that tree of Life which grew in the midst of the garden of Eden.

The staple product of this land is sugar. A certain amount of coffee is grown, and cocoa and rice, &c., but sugar is king. This fact explains what is meant by "plantations" and "estates," into which the three provinces of Essequebo, Demerara, and Berbice are largely divided. But I shall tell you more about these later on.

We have also our villages, some of which are very picturesque and thriving. One of the nicest that I have seen so far is Sandvort. It is about three miles distant from New Amsterdam, and about

THE LAND WHERE SUGAR GROWS

two miles from a place called "Orange," so named on account of the number of orange trees that used to grow there. A walk along the forest paths, or through the village garden, if one may call it such, shows us new plants and flowers at every turn. Birds of gorgeous plumage sit upon the branches of the trees, some yellow, some a deep dark red, some ruby, some white, some maroon, some black; and beautiful many-coloured butterflies flit from leaf to leaf and flower to flower, all adding to the intensity and beauty of the scene.

Such walks, however, must be taken in the daytime, and even then with care, for insects and reptiles, and even savage animals, lurk among the shrubs and flowers. Even we in the town are sometimes disturbed by "tigers," jaguars, cammoudi, snakes &c. A week or two ago, our local paper, *The Gazette*, contained the following paragraph: "A labba tiger was shot in the promenade gardens on Tuesday afternoon. Some visitors saw the animal in the heat of the day, lying comfortably on one of the garden seats, but as soon as it saw them it ran up one of the trees. An alarm was raised, and Lieut. Swain, who had been made aware of the presence of the beast, shortly put in an appearance armed with a gun. The tree was not very high where the tiger was, and, taking good aim, he shot the intruder through the head. The tiger measured four feet within four inches, and stood a foot and a half high" (*Gazette*, June 27, 1896). A month later, July 22nd, the same paper contained a short account of an alligator attacking a coolie boy in one of our villages and dragging him into the water. The following is the account of the incident: "A coolie boy was lying on the bank of the trench with his hand in the water, when it was seized and he was dragged into the trench. Soomanah, a coolie woman, heard his scream, and seeing him in the trench thought he had got out of his depth whilst bathing, so she jumped in after him, then she gave vent to a series of deeply religious objurgations, terminating with '*Alligator.*' This, Mr. Wrong says he heard, the trench being close to his house, and he ran from his bed (he had fever) to the trench, where he found the woman's clothes enfolding the alligator, and her natural position reversed, her head being in the mud. He jumped upon the alligator, grasping its neck, and trying to tread it down with his feet, but at last he had to grasp the upper and lower jaws and tear them open before the brute let go its victim. The boy's arm was mangled and broken above the elbow. The reptile sank in deep water and disappeared."

THE LAND WHERE SUGAR GROWS

About the people of this land, their callings and customs, their manners and morals, their races and religions, I must tell you in another chapter. Suffice it to say that it is a land as yet in its infancy, but it has in it the elements of growth, and of greatness.

> "There are many things in the womb of Time
> Yet to be delivered."

IV

THE HISTORY OF A POUND OF SUGAR

"DO you take sugar in your tea?" asked the lady at the head of the table, in a soft musical voice and with a pleasant smile upon her face.

"Madam, I like all sweet things," I replied; "I like a sweet face, a sweet disposition, a sweet child, and a sweet *lady*, madam, like you."

"You are complimentary, I perceive," she said.

"Compliments help to sweeten life, and we should never withhold them where they are due. The present example is a case in point. But may I ask you what kind of sugar this is?"

"This is what is called Demerara Crystals," she said, "but you would not believe what a difficulty I have had in procuring it. Brown sugar and what is called raw sugar you can get at any grocer's shop. But in most cases this is sugar made from beetroot, and coloured to make it look like the sugar which comes from the sweet cane. Few housekeepers here know the respective values of these two sugars. Indeed, like most things of everyday use, people get them and seldom make any inquiry about them."

"Madam, I am so pleased to hear you speak thus. I wish we had more ladies who inquire into, and interest themselves in, the products that are put upon our tables. Each one of these products has a history, and results that are not only national but worldwide often follow our choice or rejection of them. As a great door hangs upon little hinges, so great events turn upon little things. Some lady who leads the fashions in Paris substitutes alpaca as a dress material for silk. This is quickly followed by the Courts of Europe and the aristocracy. Their example is copied by all the other classes of society. The result is that the silk industry is ruined. The mills at Macclesfield and Congleton and Derby first run short time and then stop. The workmen have no work, the children cry for bread; homes are broken up, and fathers and mothers have to go forth to seek a new home and a new employment. This kind of thing is going on constantly. Change brings change. Electricity is being substituted for gas here. Already the gas shares have gone down fifty per cent., and a number of men are thrown out of employment. Society is like rows of bricks set on end and leaning one upon another; when one falls a number fall with it. Cane sugar was once the dominant sweetener. It had the field all to itself. It reigned without a rival there. But during the Napoleonic wars with England, France and Germany could not get their sugar from the West Indies as before, and so Napoleon had sugar made from beetroot. That sugar most of our English people use, not because it is better, but because it is, as they think, a little cheaper. But in this they are very much mistaken, for the cane sugar has double the sweetening power of beetroot sugar. One pound of Demerara crystals will sweeten as much as two pounds of white or brown beetroot. In addition to this there are the wholesome qualities of the cane juice. During the sugar harvest, black boys and girls, and even black men and women and coolies, may be seen walking along the road with a long stick of sugarcane in their hands, often chewing away at it with pleasure and satisfaction. Indeed, as Dr. Brewer says, 'Every creature, whether man or animal, during the sugar harvest appears to derive benefit from its use and becomes fat and healthy.'"

THE HISTORY OF A POUND OF SUGAR

"Will you tell us," said the lady of the house, "how this sugar is made? The children have just been saying how much they would like you to give them a history of it."

"It is always a pleasure, madam, to gratify your desires, providing, as Sir Walter Scott says, 'they be virtuous,' and as for these children—bless their sweet faces—who could refuse them anything? Now, children, you know, if we want to understand the history of a thing we must go back to the very beginning; and to get back to the beginning of this thing, Demerara sugar, we must take ship and sail away about 4,500 miles to a land called British Guiana. And a very wonderful land in many respects it is. It is a land of perpetual sunshine and perpetual summer. We might say of it—

"'There is a land, a sunny land,
Whose skies are ever bright.'

Frost and fog, snow and ice are unknown. No chilling blast invades this clime; it is always genial, bright, and hot. The trees are always green, the flowers always bloom, the birds and butterflies are always on the wing.

"It is also a land of large rivers, of mixed races, of dense forests and of immense savannahs. Birds of gorgeous plumage fly through the air and jump from twig to twig; the ground at night becomes star-bespangled with myriads of electric fireflies; insects everywhere whistle and sing. It is a land of sweet-smelling flowers, of luscious fruits, of milky nuts, and many other things that are pleasant to the eyes and sweet to the taste.

"But it is of the sweet cane I want to tell you. It is very ancient, for we read of it in some of the early books of the Bible. The prophet Isaiah (xliii. 24), speaking for Jehovah, complains that Israel had not honoured God with his sacrifices and offerings, and he says, 'Thou hast bought me no sweet cane with money.' And Jeremiah says (vi. 20), 'To what purpose cometh there to me incense from Sheba, and the sweet cane from a far country?' From these passages we learn that the sugarcane was grown in Palestine some three thousand years ago as well as in other countries, and was often brought as an offering unto God. Between those days of three thousand years ago and these a considerable difference exists, but the sugarcane is practically the same.

"Nearly all the cultivated portion of British Guiana is devoted to the growth and production of the sugarcane. All the land on the seacoast is divided into estates or plantations. Each of these plantations contain from five hundred to two thousand acres. It is one of the beautiful sights of the country to see these plantations when the cane has grown and is in full bloom; and it is also very interesting to see the labourers at work in the fields, some ploughing, some planting, some weeding, and some trashing. A sugar estate is always a place of varied activity. In connection with it is a 'mill' for the grinding of the canes and the making of sugar. In this mill very costly machinery is used, and thousands upon thousands of pounds are invested in this sweet industry. By the kindness of one of the managers we will now go over the sugar plantation, and begin at the very beginning.

"And first of all there is the *land*. That is the basis of all our operations. We cannot value it too much or prize it too highly. Have you ever thought of it, that everything we have comes out of the land? Labour and land are the two great producers. All our wealth comes from the union between these two."

"What," says Arthur, "does everything come from the land?"

"Yes. Here is this table, made out of a tree of the forest. Here is this white cloth, it is made out of the inner bark of the flax. Here are the cups and saucers made out of the clay. Your woollen jacket comes from the back of a sheep that feeds on the land, your boots from the skin of the ox or the horse; all our calicoes are made out of cotton that grows on the trees; our tea, our sugar, our butter, our bread, all come out of the land. The land is the ever fruitful source of all our supplies, and the land, or 'the earth, is the Lord's and the fulness thereof.'

"The first thing to be done with the land, says the overseer, is to clear it and drain it. In order to do that thoroughly, and have a supply of fresh water in the time of drought, we dig these large trenches round and across the fields. We then begin planting. We take the tops of cane and plant them closely together in rows. These rows have to be six feet apart. In that field there, you see a number of black women and girls and coolies at work. They have hardly anything on, for the sun is very hot. If a kind Providence had not protected their heads with a strong thick covering of wool, they could not have stood out under the burning rays of that sun. There they will work for a whole day, and at the end of the day they will have earned 'two bits,' that is eightpence. When the canes have grown to the height of about two feet the soil is thrown up on the roots; this is done by a shovel or fork and is called ploughing.

THE HISTORY OF A POUND OF SUGAR

This is to be done as occasion requires, and the ground is to be kept clear of grass and weeds; this is called weeding. In about fifteen months the canes have grown to the height of five and six feet, the 'arrows' appear, and they are ready for cutting. Then comes the harvest. It requires a strong arm to cut those canes. This is usually done by black men. They are much stronger than the coolies and can get through more work. For cutting the canes they get from 48 cents a day. The stumps of the canes left in the earth spring up again. These are called ratoons, and at the end of twelve or thirteen months they are ready for the harvest. The canes have to be cut as near the ground as possible, because the richest juice is found in the lower joints. After they are cut, the canes are conveyed to the factory in iron punts that are drawn by mules up the trenches. They are then placed in a machine called the 'crusher,' which consists of two very heavy and powerful rollers. These rollers will weigh from five to six tons each, and are made of the best wrought-iron. From 100 lbs. of canes, 65 lbs. to 75 lbs. of cane juice will be expressed or squeezed out. This juice, which is of a sweetish taste and of the colour of dirty water, passes at once into a small reservoir, where it usually receives a dose of quicklime, and without delay runs off to large iron or copper vessels, which are heated by steam pipes. As the temperature of the juice rises, a thick scum forms on the top; this is either removed by skimming, or the juice is drawn off from below. It then passes into other pans, which are heated by fires under them, and as it is made to boil and bubble the impurities rise to the surface and are removed. After it has been clarified and reduced to a certain consistency by heat, it is drawn off into what is called the 'vacuum pan.' This is a large cylindrical copper pan, from nine feet to twelve feet in diameter, heated to about 150°F. Inside this the juice is whirled round, and as it proceeds, crystals begin to form. When it is sufficiently thick it is run out into coolers, and the liquid that comes from this is called molasses or treacle. The sugar is then packed off into bags or hogsheads. After that it is taken to the wharf and shipped to those countries where it is needed. So, you see, that sugar with which you sweeten your tea was once the juice or the sap running up the little pipes or ducts of the sugarcane; and black men and women from Africa, and red men and women from India, and yellow men and women from China, and Portuguese and English have all been employed to get you that sugar with which you sweeten your delightful cup of tea."

MISSION HOUSE, N. A. BERBICE.

[To face p. 65.

V

IN A TROPICAL HOUSE

ONE of the first things that strikes you on going ashore, and especially if it be night and the rainy season, is the hissing, whistling, and croaking sounds that fill the air. You could fancy yourself in some factory with the machinery running at full speed. This is caused by the insects that creep out in the darkness, like one of old "seeking whom they may devour." Their name is Legion. In addition to the mosquitoes, which, like the poor, "ye have always with you," we have the black beetles, known by the name of cockles and hardbacks; also cockroaches, and grasshoppers, and locusts, the sawyer beetle, the scissors-grinder, the great borer, the stag-horn beetle, the candle fly, the maribuntas, and a whole host beside which set up their nightly music. In addition to these there are the swarms of frogs that infest the wayside, the roads, and the trenches.

> "Frogs to the right of you,
> Frogs to the left of you,
> Frogs in front of you
> Whistle and croak."

Big frogs with big bass voices that can be heard one or two miles away, and little ones that whistle and wheeze, all in a chorus of their own. As my wife said, "This is the very paradise of insects." The insect concert commences at dusk. At that time the performers begin to tune their instruments. There is a beetle called here "*the six o'clock beetle*," that leads off the entertainment. He might be called the conductor. With a shrill whistle he sounds the keynote; the others take it up, and soon the music is in full fling.

Having piloted our way through these hordes of insects, but not without many a sting and blister, we arrive at a tropical house. These houses are very different from what we are accustomed to at home. They are built entirely of wood.

As you will notice from the picture, they stand on brick or wooden pillars about eight feet from the ground. This at once secures them from the damp, which at certain seasons of the year is very considerable; also from the crawling reptiles and

IN A TROPICAL HOUSE

the buzzing insects. It also lifts them from the miasma which, in the night season, rises to a height of about six feet. To get into these houses you have to ascend a flight of steps from the outside, so that you are literally always living upstairs. Running along the front of the house is the verandah, or gallery. This is sometimes open, but more frequently closed in with three or four windows and jalousies. These jalousies are an arrangement of wood made on the principle of a venetian blind, which you can open or shut at pleasure. When open they let in the breeze, at the same time excluding the sun. When closed they exclude both rain and light. The gallery, or verandah, is the coolest part of the house. There we sit and meet our friends, the pleasant cool breeze fanning our cheeks and modifying the otherwise oppressive heat of the sun. A tropical house has, of necessity, many windows. The one I am now writing in has thirty; some have twice that number. These windows are, for the most part, wide open during the day, letting a current of cool air blow freely through every room. In England we are accustomed to see chimneys on the top of every house. Who would think of building a house without a chimney? But here the houses are without chimneys. We do not need them, for we have no fireplaces in any of our rooms. At home, when you go into the breakfast-room or the drawing-room you sit by the fire. But when you come out here, you do not know which way to sit at first; you may turn any way you like, but after a while you naturally sit with your face to the breeze.

"If you have no fires," you say, "how do you cook your food?" Well, that is an important question, for we cannot, as Carlyle says the Tartars do, make our steak ready by riding on it. The kitchen or cooking-place is a little room adjoining the house. There the sable cook prepares all our food, sometimes in an American or English stove, and if you be poor and cannot afford one of these, in what is called a "coal-pot." The fuel used is wood, which can be got in large quantities from the forest. When you enter a house in England after a long journey, one of the first things that a hospitable hostess asks you to do is to "come upstairs and wash yourself." There you go into the bathroom, and you have only to turn the tap and either hot or cold water comes at your call. But here we have no water in our houses. Taps are an unknown thing, unless it be the tap at the rum-shop. And yet a good wash in clean, cool water is even more necessary and more refreshing in a hot country than a cold one. If you have been out you come home heated, perspiration oozing out at every pore, your hands, your face, your neck, your whole body wet and sticky; a bath after this is quite a luxury. But where must we get the water? We have no reservoirs, no river-water that is fit, no mountain lakes. But we have the fountain that supplies all these, namely, the clouds and the rain. The water that falls in showers upon our houses is conducted, by means of pipes, into large vats. Every good house and every large building has its vat. In these vats the best of water, that which comes down direct from heaven, is stored, and from these we draw our supplies.

On going into the bedroom you will be surprised to see the bed enclosed by a thin white netting; this is to keep out the mosquitoes. It is securely fastened at the top, and tucked in under the mattress at the bottom. When you want to get into bed, you look round to see that there are no "misskitties" near; then pulling out the curtain, you jump in and tuck it under again quick; then sitting up and looking round, you feel very much like a bird in a cage. These mosquito curtains are very necessary and a great comfort—not only as preservatives against these stinging insects, but for keeping out rats, and bats, and centipedes, and tarantuli, &c. One night I woke up to find that a bat had in some way got under my netting and into my bed. Now bats I do not like; they are too much like a mouse and too little like a bird. And of all places I certainly do not like one in bed. I went for the creature, but as the Scotchman would say, "it gaed oot o sicht." We have many bats here, and some of a very large kind. The vampyre bat sometimes measures two or more feet across the wings. These bats are called blood-suckers, for they approach a sleeping person and, without waking him, puncture some vein and drink the blood. Some children living in the interior have been known to be quite pale, weak, and emaciated from loss of blood in this way. I myself once woke up to find my leg covered with blood from this same cause. Another creature to be dreaded is the centipede. These creatures have forty-two legs and eight eyes; but what is more important still, they have a venomous bite. The natives here are much afraid of them, and they say " If centipede bite you, you must get fever." These creatures hide in the corners and crevices of the houses, and especially in old houses. I have seen them crawling up the mosquito curtains, and more than once they have dropped out of my pants as I took them up to put them on. In fact it

IN A TROPICAL HOUSE

is necessary here to give all your clothes a good shake before putting them on. A lady will find one in the folds of her skirt, and inside the slipper seems a favourite resort for them. One lady that I knew, whilst busy at her toilet, felt something crawling on her shoulder; she screamed and called her husband, and he had just time to knock the centipede off before biting her in the neck. One day whilst I sat at dinner in a friend's house, I felt something crawling up my leg. Gripping it through my trousers. I said "Excuse me," and walked off, holding it tightly, into a private room; there pulling up my trousers slop, I found a large centipede, but my firm grip had effectually prevented its bite and its sting.

Another very troublesome insect is the "chigor," or "jigger" as it is called here—*Pulex penetrans*, the "penetrating flea." You do not see them, they are so small, but you feel them. They chiefly attack the feet, and seem to be very fond of the fleshy part of the toes. My first experience of them was as follows. One night I felt a peculiar itching sensation under one of my toes. And, as Burton says in his "Anatomy of Melancholy," "a man must needs scratch where it itches." So to work I went. Next day it was pretty much the same; then I found a kind of white spot, and the symptoms got worse. On asking the old black nurse about it, she said, "Oh, parson, dat am de jigger," and she began to explain. I said, "Well, I'm jiggered! But it must come out." So a stocking-needle was produced and they began to poke away at this poor toe till they had got a hole in about the size of a pea, and out of that they pulled a bag-like nest which the chigoe had formed and in which it had laid its eggs. Rubbing some tobacco-dust in the wound, which made me dance for a few moments, it soon got all right. You will now understand the native proverb, "Me bin a good dance man, but chiggah 'pile me foot." But I must not weary you with these stories. If you are at home in England, go to your bed and, as you lie there, thank God that you do not see the rats "playing hide-and-seek" and "leap-frog" around your bed, and that there are no cockroaches in the folds of your pillow, waiting for a favourable opportunity to get near you and pick your teeth.

Life in the tropics is very different from life in the temperate zone. Our days and nights are about equal all the year round. It comes light about a quarter before six, and at that time we are astir. The little black butler brings you upstairs a cup of Berbice coffee. As soon as it is brought into the room you smell it. It is just like a posy; its aroma fills the house. We could not get on without our "cawfee in de marnin'," as you will see from the song of poor old Jane.

"Some people likes de choklet, some people likes de tea,
  Some drinks de sugar-watah, and some de lemonade;
But I ca'e fo' none o' dose, de only t'ing fo' me,
  Is me bowl o' bilin' cawfee in de marnin'.

I'se an ole woman now and does often punis' haad,
  But I'se had me good days, and I mus' satisfy;
I can still hol' togedder and still praise de Laad,
  If I only gets me cawfee in de marnin'.

Sometimes I has it grand wid me sal'fish and me fat,
  And de yellow-plantain biled, and green peppa and some rice;
But what me mind does gi'e me fo', mo' better dan all dat,
  Is me cawfee wid a gill-bread in de marnin'.

Wid de gun-fire I gets up ebery marnin', dry or wet,
  So as neber to be lated fo' de work I has to do;
And I gen'lly says me praye's—unless I does fo'get,
  But I always drinks me cawfee in de marnin'."

(From the *Argosy*.)

Along with the coffee is a little bread and butter or a little toasted cassava cake, which is an excellent repast. After this we have our bath, pouring the water over the body with the "calabash," which makes a splendid substitute for an earthenware pot. Our toilet being finished, we get downstairs to our work. By seven o'clock the streets of the town are quite busy, and from that time on, the "stores" are in full fling. This being the cool part of the day, the Europeans often avail themselves of it to walk abroad, and it is not unusual for calls to be made even at that early hour. Breakfast is taken from ten to eleven, and in some respects is a more substantial meal than the one taken in England. Fish is plentiful, and we have some excellent kinds. The queriman, sometimes called the "Guianese salmon," is a fish not unworthy of that name. Fried queriman steaks, or gillbacher, or snapper, we can get five mornings out of seven, and at a very reasonable price. To fish we have, as a rule, "rice" and yam, and cassava, and sweet potato, and plantain. About two, we take a little fruit for lunch. And of this we have a great variety and plentiful supply. Our houses, as a rule, are surrounded by fruit trees. Just under one of my windows is an orange tree loaded with Seville oranges, and a few yards from it, under another window, is a lemon tree, its branches bending under the weight of the large green lemons. Right opposite where I write is a pomegranate tree, also full of fruit. Then we have mango trees, and guava trees, and star-apples, and cocoanut trees, and bananas, and sappodillas,

A COOLIE FAMILY.

SELLING FISH IN GEORGETOWN.

[To face p. 74.

and granodilloes, and pines, besides many others; so that we are never at a loss for fruit. Spiced mangoes are a special favourite just now, and bananas, so soft and juicy, are always nice. A lady's finger of the ruddy-skinned banana, when offered by a lady, who could refuse? Pineapples fresh cut we can often get; "half a bitt" will sometimes purchase one in the country, and a "bitt" in the town. The other day we had a fine water-melon sent to us by a lady; it must have been twelve or fourteen inches long, and weighed as many pounds.

Dinner hour is about seven. By that time the heat of the day is over and you feel more inclined to eat. The usual course is soup—and they are excellent soup makers in this country. A good cook will give you a fresh kind of soup for every day in the week. "Foo-foo" soup is a great favourite amongst the people. It is a soup into which they put pounded plantains made into little balls. After soup comes fish, then fowl, or a roast, then pudding, and a cup of tea to "loose the talking ganglions and aid digestion." Of course I have described an ordinary dinner for the middle class. There are those who add to this, and those who have to subtract. Some never begin either breakfast or dinner without their swizzle, their cocktail or their "Morning Glory"; whilst others, again, have to be satisfied with a good dish of foo-foo and vegetables. It is here as in other places—

> "Some ha' meat that canna eat,
>   And some can eat that want it ;
> But we ha' meat, and we can eat,
>   And so the Lord be thankit."

VI

IN A TROPICAL CITY

HAVING given you some account of the house and the way we live, let us now go outside and look around us. This is the city of Georgetown, the finest city in the whole of the West Indies. It stands at the mouth of the river Demerara. This river is called by the Spaniards "Rio-de-Mirara"—the wonderful river, and by the Dutch "Demerary," from *Demirar*—the wonderful. The source of this river has not yet been explored. Away in the interior, not far from the equatorial line, it is supposed to have its origin in two small streams. Its course is from south-east to north-west. At its mouth it is about two miles broad, and sheltered from every wind. Bell, in his "Geography," says: "It is never visited by those tremendous hurricanes so frequent in tropical countries, and so destructive in the

West Indian Islands; it forms one of the finest harbours in the world, and could with ease contain the whole navy of Great Britain." Unfortunately, however, a bar of sand stretches across its mouth, over which no vessel drawing more than nine feet of water can pass until half-flood. At high water in spring tides, when the bar is covered to the depth of eighteen feet, larger vessels can pass, but they still require very cautious navigation. The water of this river is very muddy, being about the colour of pea-soup, and the sea for many miles round is tinged with the same hue. Up above the falls, however, the water is fresh, and its colour very clear. Good-sized vessels can run up a distance of about seventy-five miles, and smaller ones a little further. Then their progress is stopped by the cataracts. Some of these are very large and difficult to overcome. It is a river that in many respects is to be dreaded. On account of the number of sharks, it is dangerous for any one to venture into it. Its current is very rapid and powerful, and the under-currents are equally strong. Sailors or boatmen who happen to fall into it are seldom seen again. The strong under-current carries them down and away, and the voracious monsters soon make them an easy prey.

IN A TROPICAL CITY

The harbour, which is the mouth of the river itself, is a spacious one, and it is a beautiful sight to see the ships of all kinds riding at anchor. Schooners and brigs ready to start out, some to the rivers that flow through the interior, to the gold diggings, and the wood-cutting grants, and the distant sugar plantations, and others to the nearest of the West Indian islands—Trinidad, Grenada, Barbadoes, &c., whilst others are off to New Amsterdam and Surinam. The larger steamships that ply between America and Canada and Great Britain give an appearance of activity and commercial prosperity to the scene. Once a fortnight the West Indian royal mail arrives, bringing its freight of letters and passengers from the homeland. And every now and then large sailing vessels enter the port from India, with their living freight of coolies for the sugar plantations; and large ice ships from America with a plentiful supply of that cool and delicious commodity, which can be bought all the year round at one cent per pound. Indeed, ice is almost as common here as at the North Pole. In addition to the ice, these ships bring a plentiful supply of fresh vegetables and fruit and fresh meat, kept cool and nice by the refrigerators and in the ice chambers.

The city of Georgetown to-day is a very different place from what it used to be. Like most places, it has had its day of small beginnings. Rome was not built in a day. As every oak tree was once an acorn, so Georgetown was once a single street. About the beginning of this century, two rows of isolated buildings, with a grass plot between them for a road, ran in an easterly direction towards the bush. These rows of houses were called Stabroek, and they were the nucleus from which this large and magnificent city has sprung. Any one walking up "Brick Dam" to-day would hardly identify it as the Stabroek of a hundred years ago; yet so it is. The Rev. J. V. P. Bronkhurst, writing in 1883, says: "Those who knew Georgetown as it was twenty years ago would hardly know it for the same place." So great has been the improvement, and so radical the changes.

Any one stepping ashore from the old world at once notices how different everything is around him. He is no longer in a city belted by the temperate zone, where the houses are built of stone, and people walk about heavily clad and muffled up. A top-coat out here is a rarity. Indeed, one would sometimes be glad to dispense with a coat altogether. A man soon finds out that he is in an atmosphere where clothes are not

needed, save for decency's sake, and are sometimes a positive inconvenience. When a European comes out here, at first, especially if he be an Englishman or a Scotchman, you will see him walking down the street at a good brisk pace, as much as to say to the natives who are loitering along, " Wake up there and look alive; are you all going to a funeral?" But after a few months he tones down. He finds that the home pace won't do out here. A man has to learn to take things "cool."

As soon as we have walked down the stelling, where the ship lands us, we find ourselves in Water Street. This street runs parallel to the river. It is a business thoroughfare. Here the " merchants most do congregate." A view of it presented helps to give some idea of its buildings and extent. At one end stands the market with its prominent tower. It was built about fifty years ago and cost 57,000 dollars. It is a fine building, replete with stalls, offices, shops, and enclosed with handsome iron railings. A walk through the market in the early morning is interesting, comic, and instructive. There you see all kinds of people and all kinds of things. Men and women of different colours and different nationalities are walking about—Indians from Madras, Calcutta, or Bombay; they have not yet cast off their native dress, in their eastern costume they jostle against you; Chinese with their peculiar round faces, their long pigtails, and their "baggy breeks" are fresh from the Celestial Empire; negroes of all shades of black, some from Africa, but most of them born in the colony, are looking and laughing and grimacing; Portuguese from Madeira and the Azores; and occasionally an Englishman and a "braw laddie," from "beyont the Tweed." Sometimes the interest is heightened by a group of almost naked Indians from the interior. These have a few curiosities to barter, and perhaps a parrot or two and a monkey, the latter being only a little less bewildered than they. As to the language that is being spoken, you would think yourself in the tower of Babel itself. It is a confusion of tongues, out of which comes a kind of broken English, and business is done. There is one peculiarity out here in the marketing, and that is, it has to be done in the early morning. Soon after six o'clock all the black cooks of the city and the poorer people have to go to the market. The meat and provisions must be bought for the day. They are then fresh, but if not got and cooked they will be bad in a few hours. Every day has to have its own supply; so every morning cook meets with cook, and they have a nice little gossip in their own innocent way.

COOKIE HAVING A GOSSIP ON THE WAY.

It would take too long to tell of all the interesting things to be seen in that market. Chief among them all are the vegetables, fruits, and flowers. Tropical vegetables are very numerous, and very different from those which we find at home. Amongst them standing pre-eminent as an article of food are the plantains. These, when full-grown but unripe, supply the place of bread, being roasted or boiled. When ripe they are a soft, sweet, yellow pulp, and are eaten by way of dessert either boiled, fried, or roasted in the husk. These plantains form the staple diet of the poorer people out here. Pounded and put in soup, they make an excellent dish called "foo-foo." Large bunches of plantains weighing from fifty to a hundred pounds are seen upon the stalls. Then there are white yams and buck yams, bitter and sweet cassava, tannias, and eddoes, sweet potatoes, pumpkins, squashes, breadfruits, ochroes, papaws, egg-plants, &c. Among the fruits are to be seen bananas, pineapples, mangoes, limes, sappodillas, star apples, mamee apples, sugar apples, custard apples, soursops, granadillas, simitoes, guavas, avocado pears, water melons, grapes, sweet oranges, Seville oranges, citrons, shaddocks, the forbidden fruit, &c., &c. Of flowers there are an immense variety—roses, ferns, begonias, orchids, jessamines, crotons, lilies, Victoria regias, &c. A fuller description of all these must be reserved for another chapter.

Leaving the market and passing along Water Street, we find ourselves in the midst of the stores. These stores are like large warehouses. There is not much display outside, but a wonderful variety of wealth within. Each store is, not a single shop, but a *nest* of shops. It is a combination of different departments. The hardware and the smallware, and the drapery, and the grocery, and the tailoring, and the furnishing, and the boot and shoe departments—all under one roof. You walk from one department to another, and whatever you need can as a rule be supplied. There are goods from Britain, from America, from Canada, from China, from India, and from nearly every part of the world. Stock to the value of ten or even twenty thousand pounds is sometimes found in one of these stores. One peculiarity about our currency here is that whilst we use for the most part English money, chiefly silver, we reckon everything in dollars and cents. The price of an article is one dollar and twenty cents, say ; you have to translate that into its English equivalent, viz., five shillings. To a foreigner this is sometimes a little perplexing, but one soon gets into it, and reckoning then becomes easy. The poorer people have different names for some of the coins. For example, a penny they call a "gill," and a fourpenny piece a "bitt," and a halfpenny a cent. You ask a hawker the price of a thing and he says, "Five gills and a bitt and a cent," that is ninepence-halfpenny. For a fowl he wants "five bitts and three gills," that is one shilling and elevenpence. Some of them make a difference between what they call a dollar and a "round dollar," the round dollar being four shillings and the dollar four shillings and twopence. The notes issued by the banks are five-dollar notes, equal to one pound and tenpence, and ten, twenty, fifty, or a hundred-dollar notes.

Open trams drawn by mules run on different routes through the city. These are driven by black men and coloured men. Black policemen in white coats parade the streets; black women, black babies, black boys and girls, all tend to give a strange aspect to the scene. The large building at this end of the picture with the tower is the post-office, and in the same building on the upper story is the library connected with the "Royal Agricultural and Commercial Society," and in another room adjoining is the museum. These places are full of interest and well repay a visit.

Following this street out with a little curve to the right, we enter the district called Kingstown. There we see the lighthouse, a very useful, if not imposing, structure. It is built of brick, and has an iron roof and gallery. Its height is about a hundred feet. At night a powerful fixed light is burned, which may be seen many miles off. This lighthouse is in communication with the lightship, which is anchored at the "bar" of the river, and from which vessels coming to Georgetown procure a pilot. The arrival of a steamship is signalled by the firing of a gun.

Kingstown is one of the nicest and healthiest parts of the city. A grand sea-wall has been built at an enormous cost, and on the top of it is a splendid promenade. Civilians find recreation and renewed health by taking a constitutional on this delightful promenade. The grand outlook over the sea, with the soft, cool breeze fanning your cheeks, the beautiful palm trees behind, and the strains of music from the band which plays at certain hours nearly every day, help to quiet the restive mind and drive dull care away. Many a white face have I seen lost in pensive thought; the young soul dreaming of the loved ones in the homeland far away.

IN A TROPICAL CITY

> "Some have gone to lands far distant,
> And with strangers made their home ;
> Some upon the world of waters
> All their lives are forced to roam.
> Some have gone from us for ever,
> Longer here they might not stay ;
> They have reached a fairer region
> Far away, far away."

Leaving that delightful spot, we return by way of Main Street. This street runs parallel to Water Street—indeed, all the streets run at right angles to each other, *i.e.*, north and south, east and west. In this street are to be found some of the finest tropical residences. Indeed, you can hardly call it a street in the sense in which that word is used at home. It is more like the entrance to a park. Grand villa residences of various styles of architecture, some with a tower and others with a cupola three or four stories high, and all of them surrounded with a garden, line the street on both sides. A great, broad, fresh-water trench runs up the centre ; its banks lined with trees, give a shade and an appearance of coolness that is refreshing. The water is covered with the magnificent Victoria regia, the leaf of which is shaped like a "frying-pan," and is sometimes two and three feet in diameter. The flower is as large as a man's head. The houses are built for coolness as well as comfort, and the wide, shady verandahs are the favourite resorts of the family. Many of the gardens are brilliant masses of colour, and the rich perfume of these tropical plants scents the surrounding air.

Running parallel with Main Street is Camp Street, a picture of which is here presented. It gives a fine view of the fresh-water trench filled with the Victoria regia. On each side, as in Main Street, are fine tropical residences; the large cabbage-palms, with a profusion of other tropical trees, making a scene which delights the eye of the observant. At the far end is the Roman Catholic Cathedral, the finest religious edifice to be found in the city.

Following this street out in the direction of the cathedral, we come to Brick Dam. This, whilst the most ancient, is also one of the most beautiful streets in the city. Carriages run along it, hardly making any noise, for you have no stone pavement here, but a hardened kind of gravel. On a base of broken granite is placed a layer of burnt earth, what the natives call "burnt dirtie"; this forms a substance like broken bricks. On the top of that is spread a layer of "caddy," or small shells, got from the seaside. This, pressed down by a steam-roller, makes a good solid road of a reddish tint.

CAMP STREET, GEORGETOWN, SHOWING TRENCH WITH VICTORIA REGIA LILIES.

The road is wide enough for three or four carriages to run abreast, and on each side is a little grass plot and beautiful tropical trees. These afford a cool and pleasant shade to the heated pedestrian. In certain months of the year, when some of the trees are in bloom, it presents the appearance of a perfect Arcadia. Here and there, on either side, is to be seen the Flambeaux, or " Burning Bush," as it is sometimes called—and the name is not inappropriate; for its flaming red leaves, with the hot sun shining upon them, give it a brilliance that few other trees possess. Its botanical name is *Poinsettia pulcherrima*. Then there is another —the " Acalypha," the peculiarity of which is that one part of the leaf is green and the other blood-red. " The leaf is large and almost round, with a point, measuring about twelve inches by nine; colour, dark metallic green, blotched with intense red."

Passing on beyond these we come to the " Avenue of Palms." These palm trees, tall and straight, with their feathery plumes, stand like sentinels on each side of the road, making a picture that is only to be seen to be admired.

As we are now in the vicinity of the Botanical Gardens, we might as well extend our walk and luxuriate there for a short time. These gardens, which are quite of recent formation, cover an area of about 212 acres. As you enter the large and magnificent bronzed gate, the soft breeze fans your cheek and the sweet breath of flowers fills the air, and a sacred silence reigns around. Beautiful flower-beds on each side, made still more beautiful by the neatly-trimmed lawn which surrounds them, and a profusion of strange plants and trees and flowers, at once arrest the eye. It would need a botanist and a florist to describe them, and even he could only do for the plants what the anatomist does for the human body. He could describe the different parts and their relationship to the whole, but you must see these parts together, and animated by a living soul, to know the majesty and grandeur of man. So with these plants and flowers.

Standing there, drinking in the perfume, and soothed by the soft and silent breeze, your eye gazing upon flowers and plants and lawns trimmed neat and in order, you begin to realise that the "luxuriance" of tropical life has been brought within the bounds of law and order. Nature here is no longer wild and wanton, but civilised and chaste. Her long tresses have been cut and trimmed, her exuberance directed into right channels and kept within proper bounds—in short,

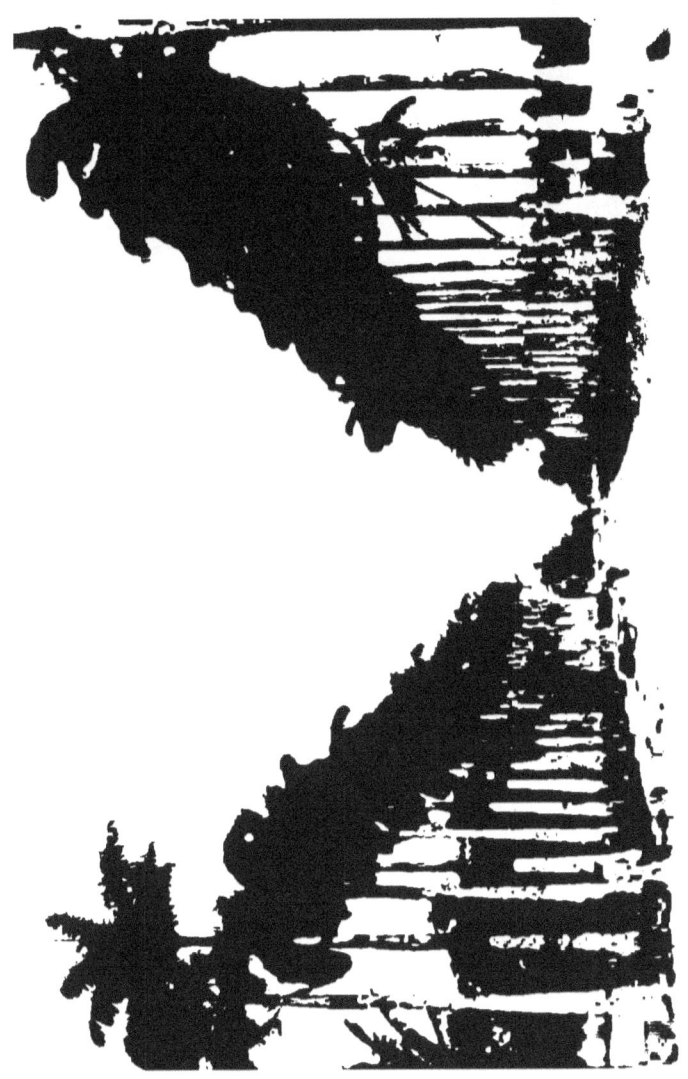

Nature has been beautified by Art. As we walked along, my friend, who himself belongs to the tropics, pointed out to me the different kinds of palm trees that are to be seen. "These two short, round trees," said he, "with the large, fan-shaped leaves, are what we call 'fan-palms' (Latania). They are fine specimens and of rare beauty. Yonder is another (Ravenalia), somewhat different. Of these there are only two kinds in the world. A peculiarity of one of these fan-palms—the 'Corypha,' I think—is that it only once flowers and then dies." How many plants there are that shed their blossoms and unfold their flowers year by year—but this one for years drinks in its nourishment, energises, and grows, gradually coming to maturity and ultimate perfection in its flower, then its work is done, the purpose of its existence is fulfilled—its leaves wither, the whole tree droops and dies. We, too, have an ultimate perfection to attain to—we may blossom here, but the full flowering of the *genus homo* lies beyond.

"These tall, straight trees, rising to a height of fifty or seventy feet, as you know," said my friend, "are the 'cabbage-palms.' Their trunk stands like a huge pillar, without a single branch till within a few feet of the top, where a kind of huge feathery plume sways to the breeze.

"Now those on the other side, though very similar, are what are called the 'royal-palm.' There is a difference, you will notice, in the trunk. The trunk of the royal-palm is shaped like a bottle—bulges out in the middle; whilst the cabbage-palm is straight and almost of equal thickness, tapering a little towards the top.

"There, with that prickly stem, is the palm 'Coquirita.' This produces a nut that is not unpleasant eating, if you are hungry and lost in the bush.

"Then there is the 'Ita' palm, as useful as it is beautiful.

"But we shall not get through these gardens to-day, if I am to explain all these peculiar plants to you. There are three, however, that I must not omit. One is the 'snow plant,' which looks as if snow had fallen upon its leaves. It is a low, bushy plant, but all its green leaves are dotted with white. Then there is the 'Quisqualis,' or 'Character d'homme,' as it is sometimes called. Its flowers are noted for changing from red to white, and on account of this changeableness it is supposed to resemble the character of men. This, of course, must have come from the ladies!

"There is another peculiar plant, called 'The

Lady of the Night.' It bears long, large tubular pendent scented white flowers in great abundance. These flowers are shut up during the day, it is said, and open as soon as night sets in, sending forth a rare fragrance and perfume to enrich the dewy eve; hence its name 'The Lady of the Night.'" We strolled on down the long avenue of trees, towards the "Lamaha" canal, admiring the massive silk cotton trees, and the sand-box trees, with their large spreading branches in some places forming a perfect covering of leaves over our head; then we entered and sat down in one of the rustic and picturesque Benaabs which are to be found on the way, and having partaken of a little refreshment, brought up by our black boy, we entered our carriage and drove away, carrying with us some fragments of that "soul of beauty" that dwells for ever in plant and flower and tree.

Of the public buildings of the city little need be said. They are not ancient like those of Athens or of Rome; but they are beautiful, and some of them even magnificent. They serve a double purpose. They are like what we wish the ladies to be—not only ornamental, but ornamental and useful.

The Town Hall is a fine structure, and would

do credit to any city, either ancient or modern. The Law Courts remind you of the same buildings in London, and in Strangeways, Manchester. They represent the spirit of fair play and justice which is inherent in the British race. Then we have the "Court of Policy," surrounded by all the Government offices, forming a solid quadrangle of architectural beauty as well as gubernatorial power. Of churches and chapels we have a fair share, representing at least outwardly our respect for the religious spirit and religious ideas. And as Dr. Johnson said his friend Mr. Cammell (Campbell) was not a religious man, yet he never passed a church without taking off his hat, so we, at least, are not deficient in that outer respect which sacred things have a right to demand.

In this magnificent tropical city are to be found, as in all cities, the best and the worst, the highest and the lowest. There are warm hearts and hospitable roofs—places for the refreshment of the body, the culture of the mind, the enrichment and ennobling of the soul. You may have happy fellowship with man, or you may be charmed with the beauty and excellence of woman; or you may wander into the gardens and get back to Nature—she will soothe you with the music of her winds, and enchant you with the perfumed breath of her flowers; or you may go back to "Nature's God," to the spirit that animates all organisms, that breathes through all entities—the soul of beauty, the heart of love.

> "There is a lesson in each flower,
> A story in each stream and bower;
> On every herb on which you tread
> Are written words which, rightly read,
> Will lead you from earth's fragrant sod,
> To hope and holiness and God."—ANON.

VII

UP TO BERBICE

IT is eight o'clock in the morning. The sun has been up some hours, and the heat is already very considerable, but as we have taken our ticket for Berbice and are already seated on the deck of a little coasting steamer called *Guiana*, we do not find it too hot.

The breeze from the sea makes it pleasant, if not cool. This steamship runs to Berbice every other day, keeping the coast line in sight all the way. The journey is performed in about seven hours. There are usually a fair number of deck passengers of different colours and races. The coolies, with their picturesque dresses, and the blacks and the mulattoes and the Chinese and the Portuguese, all sitting and chatting, make a picture in itself unique. Sometimes, if it happens to be a little rough, the ship rolls a great deal, and the big waves come tumbling over the ship's side, giving you a sea-bath whether you will or no. On the upper deck you are free from the waves, but your bones get a good shaking, and you are generally glad when you get to your journey's end.

On entering the mouth of the river Berbice, which is about two miles and a quarter broad, we find there are two channels, one to the right and the other to the left. These channels are separated from each other by a small island that has been formed by the silting up of the sand or mud.

Crab Island—for that is its name—is about a mile in circumference. It is covered with bush and small trees. It takes its name from the number and excellence of the crabs that are to be found there. During the crab season the Indians of the upper part of the river used to come a distance of from forty to two hundred miles to enjoy a feast on crabs; for the Indian is said to be passionately fond of them, and they are not to be had in such perfection in his own locality. As we sail up the eastern channel—for that is the deepest, having from seventeen to twenty feet of water at high tide—we notice the ruins of an old fort formerly known as Fort

St. Andries. This fort was built by the Dutch, having a brick paling four feet high, with a moat on the outside, and mounted with eighteen twelve-pounders. In those days it must have been a source of dread to the enemies' ships as they sought to enter the mouth of the river. Happily in these days we have no need for it. Briton's forts are floating forts; our ships of war can be concentrated on any given point for our protection, at a comparatively short notice. Our brave sea-dogs are our defence, and our own stout hearts and strong arms.

Having passed Crab Island, there is a pretty view of the river Canje, or "Canje Creek," as it is called, emptying itself into the Berbice river. This is a very considerable stream, and along its banks are to be found some thriving villages and not a few large and flourishing sugar plantations. A new iron swing bridge has just been completed at a cost of $125,000. It is 336 feet long, and has a clear roadway for traffic of 17 feet. The swing span in the centre, which turns on a single pivot, weighs about a hundred tons, and by a simple mechanical arrangement one man can lift and turn this massive iron gateway. The whole weight of the bridge, exclusive of the piling and concrete abutments, is about 2,600 tons.

It is a triumph of engineering skill, and is a credit to the engineer who was the presiding genius during its four years of building. It is the largest bridge in the colony.

We now come to the town of New Amsterdam. The view of it from the river is quite a picture. The tall palm trees, standing like sentinels, and the waving plumes of the cocoanut trees, make it look like a city of palms. Here and there a tower or a church steeple rises above the tops of the houses; and the little piers or jetties where the ships land, and the long row of merchants' stores, all in turn present themselves to the eye. There is an air of repose about the town that strikes a stranger fresh from the busy thoroughfares of an English city. And well there may be, for we may call it the *Ne plus ultra* of civilisation. Beyond! What is there? No town, no city. A few villages are to be found along the banks of the river for ten or twelve miles further on, and then you plunge into forest and bush and savannah, extending for hundreds of miles in all directions. No roads, no paths, save the track of the Indian, to lead you anywhere. You are in the "Wild Country," amongst the wild beasts and sometimes even wilder men.

As our little ship drew up to the stelling, we

found it packed with people; and as soon as the gangway was secured a great crowd of black natives rushed on board. A good old African, named John Marks, for nearly fifty years a deacon of Mission Chapel, came up to me, and taking my hand he said, "We welcome you to Berbice in de name ob de Lord"; then one and another grasped my hand—but one hand was not enough, they took both, and if there had been fifty, there would still have been some short. Then we were led down the pier, lined on each side with happy, beaming faces. Amid hurrahs and "Tank God," and "A we parson come," and "Bless de Lord," we got to the street. There we saw the roadway lined with black children and grown-up people, waving their banners and shouting. Putting us into the parson's waggon, we were driven off to Mission Chapel and the Mission House. There the big bell was ringing out its welcome; the chapel and the yard and the house were all filled; they danced, they shouted, they sang—old and young alike were carried away with the glad enthusiasm.

Reader, do you wonder why this was? Let me tell you. About eight months before, their young minister, the Rev. S. H. France, who had only been with them a little over a year, died of malarial fever. Mr. France was a talented young man, and greatly beloved by his people. He was a companion of mine in our early days and a fellow student, with others such as Dr. C. A. Berry, whose name and fame is already in two worlds. He afterwards became my brother-in-law. The people knew what a reputation British Guiana had in England for unhealthiness—a reputation I may say that, in these days, is not deserved ; and they were told no minister would risk his life to come out to them from England. Hence their enthusiasm and their joy.

That night we had a grand reception meeting. Long before seven o'clock the large edifice was packed. There would be close upon two thousand people present. The Rev. W. H. Downer and other native ministers were there. Never shall I forget how they sang that beautiful hymn :

> "We bid thee welcome in the name
>   Of Jesus our exalted Head :
> Come as a Servant ; so He came,
>   And we receive thee in His stead.
>
> Come as a Shepherd : guard and keep
>   This fold from hell and earth and sin ;
> Nourish the lambs and feed the sheep ;
>   The wounded heal, the lost bring in.
>
> Come as a Watchman ; take thy stand
>   Upon thy tower amidst the sky ;
> And when the sword comes on the land
>   Call us to fight, or warn to fly.

Come as an Angel, hence to guide
  A band of pilgrims on their way ;
That, safely walking at thy side,
  We fail not, faint not, turn, nor stray.

Come as a Teacher, sent from God,
  Charged His whole counsel to declare ;
Lift in our ranks the prophet's rod
  While we uphold thy hands with prayer.

Come as a Messenger of peace
  Filled with the Spirit, fired with love ;
Live to behold our large increase,
  And die to meet us all above."

As we have to stay in New Amsterdam some time, we will walk through the quaint little town and look about us.

And first of all we will go into the business part of the town, which is Water Street. If you expect to see rows of shops, the same as you see in England, you will be very much disappointed. There are no "shops" here. They are all *stores.* They are low one-storied buildings—save where a second story is used as a dwelling-place—and have no architectural beauty : they look like some place for warehousing goods. From the outside you never dream of the wealth and variety within. Inside, the store is divided into different departments. There is the dry goods department, the hardware, the boot and shoe, the grocery, the tailoring, the hosiery, the perfume, the furniture, the saddlery and harness departments, the book department, the salt fish and lime, the rope and twine the oil and lamp, the spirits and wine departments. In fact, you have here *multus in uno*, many things in one. To fit up one of these stores as it ought to be fitted up, would cost fifteen or twenty thousand pounds. Sometimes they will have in the store goods to the value of £10,000. Now it is clear from this that none but *large capitalists* can "run a store" of that first-class order. And this in itself is an evil. Our English system of keeping each department separate enables twenty persons, with small capital, to set up their own little business. And twenty persons, each earning £200 a year, is better for the community than one person earning the whole £4,000 a year.

But you say, "Can't a big store be worked more economically, and therefore the goods be sold much cheaper?" If we are to judge from the prices you have to pay in the stores, I should say not. The stranger coming from England is simply astounded at the price he has to pay for his commodities out here. When butter is 1s. 1d. per lb. at home he has to pay 2s. 2d. here; for his cheese he must always pay 1s. 4d. per lb., the same kind he can buy in

England at 4d. and 6d. per lb.; even sugar, which is made here and shipped, can be bought at a penny a pound less in England than here. This arises from the heavy duty put upon all imported sugar, making it, in fact, prohibitive. Nearly everything, except purely native products, is double, and in some cases treble, the price you pay at home. Great fortunes have been made, and out of nothing. But as the Creole proverb says, "Dis time no like befo' time." Competition is bringing down prices, and store-keepers, even out here, are beginning to find that they must bring themselves into line with the times.

Passing out of Water Street into Main Street, we find another busy thoroughfare, though the stores are of a somewhat smaller kind, and in and among them are dwelling-houses, some of them looking very neat and nice. And of course we have one or two rum shops.

What strikes a stranger is the peculiarity of some of the names. "Ho A Hing," and "Che A Wai," and "Edward Foo," and "Lou A Hing," and "John Fong A Fook," and "J. Lou Shee," and "Woa-Sam"—these are all Chinese store-keepers. "Ho A. Hing" is one of our most successful merchants; he came, it is said, as an indentured immigrant when a boy, and from the humblest begin-

COOKIE RETURNING FROM MARKET.

[To face p. 105.

A CHINESE WOOD-CARRIER.

ning he has worked his way to a position of eminence and opulence.

The Chinese make good shopkeepers, and as business men I have always found them easy to get on with. They have their peculiarities, but, as a rule, they make good colonists and law-abiding citizens.

New Amsterdam has three principal streets, each one being about a mile long and running right through the town in parallel lines. These are crossed at right angles by a large number of smaller streets. On each side of every street is a trench, so that there are no footpaths or sidewalks. Two-footed animals and four-footed animals alike have to take to the road. Over these trenches are little wooden bridges, like those you find in Holland. In fact, the whole system of streets and of drainage was originally carried out by Dutchmen, and is on the same plan as that which obtains in their own country.

Here is a view of Water Street. It is from a photo taken by Sheriff Hewick. The buildings on the right are stores. The tall trees are cabbage-palms, waving their feathery plumes above the tops of the buildings. The tower which we see before us is the Market Tower; it is used as a signal to incoming ships. The telegraph-poles tell us that we are not much behind in our use of electric power. Most of the well-to-do citizens and business men have the telephone in their houses. The charge is $12.00 or £2 10s. per annum. In Georgetown they have the electric light, and already negotiations are going on for the purpose of bringing it here. The patient donkey is plodding on with its load; two little black girls are going to or returning from school, and others near the market are bent on their own particular business or pleasure. On the left hand are the little bridges that span the trenches and lead to the different cross streets. Behind the palings, all the way down, are fine tropical residences, each enclosed by a garden, and surrounded by bright, many-coloured, ever verdant trees and shrubs.

The population of New Amsterdam is about ten thousand, but is greatly augmented by the influx of people from the surrounding villages. It is composed of Europeans, English, Scotch, Irish, and of Chinese, of Portuguese, chiefly from the island of Madeira, of Coolies from India, of coloured, and of native black people. With such a variety of races we find a variety of manners, dress, language, and customs. Of these I will speak after.

STRAND, N. A. BERBICE.

[*To face p. 107.*

But what do the people do? is the question often asked at home. What is the staple industry? Well, being a shipping port, there are a large number of men who find employment about the wharfs, in loading and unloading ships. Then the stores employ a number as clerks and porters. The houses being all built of wood we have a large number of carpenters; then we have boat-builders and painters, tailors and shoe-makers. Those who have no trade take to gardening, *i.e.*, they hire a piece of land and grow plantains, cassava, yams, sweet potatoes, rice, &c. These are called "farmers." Many of the women work in the field, and all around us are the sugar estates, which employ a considerable number of people; but the planters now rely chiefly upon their indentured coolies, as they do the work at a considerably lower rate.

New Amsterdam is governed by a town council, but the franchise is so exclusive that the election is almost an absurdity and a farce. We have a few public buildings that are worthy of note. The town hall, the courthouse with its Government offices, the various churches and chapels, a public almshouse, and a hospital. The latter is far away the finest building in the town. It is a beautiful design, and does credit to both the architect and the builder.

It is large, airy, spacious, and is surrounded with a fine variety of tropical plants and flowers. Its garden is well kept, and is a credit to the doctor who presides over it, and to the whole town.

Of the churches and chapels, there is a fine Anglican church which seats about 900, and a bonny little Scotch kirk which for picturesqueness takes the shine out of them all. Then there is a Roman church, a Wesleyan church, a Lutheran church, and a Congregational. The latter is known as "Mission Chapel": it was established by the London Missionary Society, and is the largest chapel in the colony. It seats 1500 people, and is an exact model of Dr. Raffles' church at Liverpool. To see it filled with an eager, interested congregation of black people is a sight to gladden a Christian minister's heart. And this is a sight I have often witnessed.

But we must now pass on, and if you will jump into my waggon (a kind of four-wheeled buggy) we will drive round to the different places of interest on the outside.

Taking the riverside way first, along which we have a road as far as plantation Highbury, *i.e.*, twelve miles, we come first of all to "Providence" estate, with its village of Islington; and just behind it, almost hidden by the sugarcanes and the trees, is the village of "Overwinning." A small tribe of "Congo Africans" occupy it, and their little thatched and wooden houses, surrounded by the large-leaved banana and plantain trees, must remind them very much of their home in Africa, from which many of them in their childhood were torn away. Standing amongst the plantain trees there is a black man and his wife ; he is over sixty years of age, and has for many years been a deacon of the London Missionary church. It is very interesting to hear him tell the story of his early life. He says: " I 'member fader and mudder too well, do (though) I was a wee picknie when de Portuguese catch me and take me 'way. De place where I libed in Africa was called Bōmah. My fader and mudder had twenty-one picknies. I was de twenty-first. And you must know in Africa if any one in debt to anoder you must pay dat debt. No matter how long, years and years and years, you still got to pay. And if you can't pay, de man come and take one ob de picknies for to pay de debt. My fader and mudder owe debt to an African man. Dey no able fo' pay, so he come and ketch me, and carry me away and sell me to some Portuguese 'man stealers.' Dey put me in chains wid a lot oders ; chain long, long, long—it fasten round a' we neck. Fifty or hundred men and boys all fasten wid dat chain. Ef one man lie down all mus' lie down. Ef one sick and no able fo' go, dey loose he, let he lie on de groun', den shoot he. De women be all fasten wid rope. We all march on, long, long way; all throo de night we walk, den we come to de ship. Dey put a' wee in de hold ob de ship, one pon anoder. Dey fasten down de hatch. We lie dere like bags ob rice, no able hardly fo' breave, so hot, hot, hot. Me cry and cry and cry. But de oders say, 'No good crying, picknie! Let we pray dat de English come and caught we, den we be all free men.' When we been sailing some time, one week, de English ship come and catch a' wee. De cap'n ob de English ship, wid his men, take de Portuguese cap'n and put him in irons, and de oder men he put in long boat; he loose a' wee and let we come up on deck, and he take wee to Serra Lone (Sierra Leone). Dere de Gubna' say, 'We be all free.' Dey send me to school; dere I learn fo' say A B C. After dat one English man come and say dey want nigger for to go to Demerara, and ef we go dey will gif us work to do in de field, and dey will gif us plenty money. One week and we sal hab a' wee beaver hat *full, full.* 'Well,' we say, 'dat is good.' Gubnah say it is true, but he no want us for go. We mus' go ef we like. So I went to de ship and came to dis colony; and on dis estate me hab libed all de time."

One of the finest roads that we have from New Amsterdam is that up the east coast. It runs in an opposite direction to the river road and keeps close by the sea. It runs right up to the Corentyne river, a distance of seventy or eighty miles. It is quite a pleasure to drive up this road on account of the openness of the country and the coolness of the breeze. On one side we have a vast savannah stretching inland for miles upon miles. Few, if any, have ever crossed it to its westward limit. Parts of this savannah are used for cattle farming and the rearing of stock. Other parts are planted with rice. Then on the other side we have the sea, it is kept back by the Courida bush, and hidden from view by a coast line of trees, but the music of its distant murmur soothes the nerves and gives quietude to the troubled mind. This east coast road is a favourite driving-place for the *elite* of the town, on account of its coolness and strong breeze. One point about two miles away, where the ladies often stop in their carriages to enjoy the breeze and have a little chat, is known by the very appropriate name of "Scandal Point," thus showing that our sisters in all parts of the world are noted for liking a little gossip.

As we drive up this way we pass through what is known as Queenstown, a kind of suburb of New Amsterdam, and then we come to the public lunatic asylum. This is a large building, surrounded by beautiful grounds. The tropical trees and flowers are lovely, and the provision grounds adjoining, which are worked and kept in order by the inmates, are a credit to the president, Dr. G. Snell, and officers of the institution. About six hundred patients are resident in this asylum. To clothe them and feed them and house them and attend to their peculiar maladies is no light task. This is done by a staff of medical men and other officers appointed and paid by the government.

The place where the asylum stands was the site of the old barracks, and close by, on the other side of the road, is the old burial ground. In that quiet place, surrounded by a clump of palm trees, many a poor fellow who left his home in the Queen's service lies sleeping. Life's battle with him is over. He has gone on his long furlough, and there he will rest till heaven's bugle sounds to call him once more into line, and to receive his reward whether it be good or whether it be evil.

Close by the asylum is the Canje bridge, over

AN EAST INDIAN BEAUTY.

which we cross, and then we come to a long line of coolie huts and wooden houses, known by the name of Sheet Anchor. Here we see the coolies in their native attire, the men often having nothing on but a girdle of cotton around their loins. Of course this is their working attire. And the women are almost as scantily clad, many of them having but a short thin skirt and a "joola," or tight-fitting bodice, which covers the bust but does not conceal it, and over the head a kind of handkerchief tied.

Away on the savannah to the left we observe a number of coolies, such as may be seen any day. They are all in their working or every-day attire. One of the females has her silvery ornaments on the wrists and arms, similar to the coolie lady in the picture. The men have put on their tunics, on seeing us approach, because, as they said, "Buckra mus' see a' wee good." The children have nothing on but their shirts, and sometimes not even these. Further up the coast we come to a row of coolie huts; and behind them are their ricefields. It is a beautiful sight to see them preparing their fields and sowing their seed; but it is a grander sight when the reaping time comes. These poor people live almost entirely on rice. They have no tables, no chairs—no furniture, indeed, of any kind.

A little four-posted settee, with a rope or wicker-work bottom, is all that they have. And this they use to sit on sometimes in the day and sleep on at night. They have no "crockery" of any kind. A calabash or a tin saucer is all that they need. They put their bit of boiled rice in this, and then, after the true eastern fashion, they dip their fingers in the dish and eat. As the black people say—"Story done."

Here is a picture of one of these coolie huts or houses. It is situated on the coast. The land on which it stands is a part of the east coast savannah. Gilall has built his little house for himself, his wife lending a helping hand. The walls are of "wattles," covered on both sides with clay. The floors are of clay, well smoothed over with a composition of clay and fine sand and besmeared with a solution of cow-dung, which gives to it a smooth appearance. The walls within and without are plastered with the same stuff. The roof is thatched with rice straw and long savannah grass. A little projection is made in front to form a kind of shade; under this awning they often sit, in coolie fashion, during the heat of the day. Windows and doors they have none. In this little family, with this little hut, we see life in its simplest and most elementary form. Their wants are few

COOLIE HOUSE, CORENTYNE COAST, BERBICE.

[To face p. 115.

and soon supplied. With love and contentment they may be happy. Without these they would not be happy, even if they possessed all things.

VIII

IN A TROPICAL CHURCH

RELIGIOUS life out here is very different from what it is at home. The underlying forces may be the same, but the expression is different. When the early Christians were filled with the Holy Ghost on the day of Pentecost they spake in different tongues. Unity of spirit and variety of expression is what we must look for. Some of the old negroes in the Rev. John Wray's time were very much exercised in their minds about this question of languages, and they waited upon him with their difficulties. One of the questions which they asked was, "Can God understand the Berbice Creoles when they pray? Or shall we have to learn English?" No; let every man speak in the tongue wherein he was born. The Creole heart, filled with the love of

PARSON AND DEACONS.

IN A TROPICAL CHURCH

God, will express itself in its simple, beautiful, Creole way.

The Sabbaths out here come upon us with a freshness and a calm that speak of God and of heaven. There is a "hush" in the soft morning breeze as it begins to blow. The stirring in the top of the palm trees tells us that God is near. There is not that rush and hurry which we so often find, even amongst our Christian people in England. Softly, softly, softly, the day dawns upon us, and the service begins. Eleven o'clock is the hour for public worship, but long before that time the people meet for prayer. In the country stations they have their little gathering at seven, and then they prepare for their journey to town. Some of them walk two, three, and even four miles to the house of God. By half-past nine these country members begin to drop in. They generally sit under the house, and quietly converse and "cool out." "Well, Buddie! How you do?" "Ou, ma'am, me been too sick; me belly hurt me too bad, and fever! hot! hot! hot! But de Lord am too good; one more time He bring me to His house. Bless His holy name." And so "sister meets with sister, and brother meets with brother, and they have fellowship one with another." At half-past ten the first bell for service begins to ring. *That* tells them it is time to start out from their homes. At a quarter to eleven the second bell begins to ring, and it rings on till a few minutes of the hour. "Come! come! come!" it seems to say. "For you God's house is open! Unto you, oh men, I call. Come! come! come! Now! now! now!" And they *do* come. From country lane and city streets they wend their way, and by eleven o'clock the church is well filled. Over a thousand people waiting to hear the Word of God! This is in itself an inspiration and a solemn call. And this is what we frequently have at Mission Chapel. Our congregations at home are impressive; but a congregation out here is both impressive and picturesque. The black faces and the dark eyes, and rows of pearly white teeth, when anything humorous is said, at once strikes the observant stranger. And then the beautiful bright colours of the ladies' dresses, and the spotlessly white collars and cuffs and large shirt fronts of the black gentlemen, all tend to make the picture before you a "thing of beauty."

Though many of the people are poor they like to dress well. The old missionaries taught them to come to God's house in their best clothes. "Put on thy beautiful garments, O

Jerusalem," means to them that they must go to church in beautiful garments. And our black young ladies, our "sable beauties," are not a whit behind their pale sisters at home. They have their light muslin dresses of white and pink and sky blue, and pale green and red and yellow; their dark hair often adorned with a sweet-smelling jessamine or a pink rose. In their hands they carry their fan and their book, whilst their feet are compressed into little high-heeled, patent-leather shoes, which contrast with the shapely white stockings. But there is a funny side also in this matter of dress. Sometimes you will see an old negress sitting boldly up in front of you with *three* hats on. First a "kerchief" round the head, worn like a turban, which they call a "tie head," then an old bonnet on the top of that, and crowning the whole some dinged and cast-off billycock, or "chimney pot." Occasionally a "Celestial" will come in; his long pig-tail hanging down behind him. The Chinese ladies wear what might be called the "divided skirt," *i.e.*, very wide trousers coming a little lower down than the calf of the leg, and over this a silk tunic. It is often very difficult to tell at first whether the Chinese before you is a man or a woman. I remember going into a shop in Trinidad kept by Woo-Shang-Hi, and I could not for the life of me tell whether the person behind the counter was a "*he*" or a "*she*." The face was smooth, the hair long and plaited, the tunic covered the breast, the voice was soft, the hands small. I said to an English boy in the shop: "Is *it* a *he* or a *she*?" "That is a man," he said; "but the lady of the shop is very much like him."

In a tropical church doors and windows are all kept wide open, so that a current of cool air is ever blowing through. In the rainy season we have sometimes to shut down the windows to keep the rain out; then the place becomes almost unbearable; the steam begins to rise from the body, and the perspiration runs down your face and neck in miniature streamlets. One of the results of these open windows is, that the preacher can be heard a long way off. Sick ones in their houses near by have thus been able to share in the blessings of the sanctuary. But whilst those outside can hear the preacher, the preacher can also hear those outside. The loud braying of a donkey close by will sometimes contest the claim of the preacher for the attention of his hearers. And it reminds one of the not-over-reverent wit, who said, "Brethren! let us bray." The negro character has not in it that modesty or shamefacedness which so often characterises their pale-faced brethren. A person at home would feel a "shame" mantling his cheek if he had to walk down the aisle of a church during service. But here the black man, or woman either, will sail down the aisle with all the dignity imaginable—head thrown back, hands spread out, measured step, conscious that all are looking at them, and, for this reason, rather liking it. Sometimes they will look round and smile, as much as to say, "Ain't I nice? Don't you admire me, Buddie?" I have seen them get up many a time during the sermon and coolly walk down the aisle to an open window to "spit," and then come back and take their seat again. But this is chiefly in our country stations.

Another thing I must mention, and that is the difficulty under which a preacher labours on account of the innumerable insects. At night, when the lamps are lit, these insects come in swarms. The mosquitoes we have always with us; but the moths, the bats, the marabunturs, and the hard-backs only come occasionally. These latter, in the rainy season, are sometimes intolerable. They come upon us in thousands and tens of thousands. The air is darkened with them. They fall on you like a shower of black hailstones, they creep through your hair, they crawl down your neck and your back, they strike you on the nose and in the eye, they crawl over your book, they get on the floor and creep up your legs, they break the lamp-glasses and put out the lights—it is like one of the plagues of Egypt. One Sunday night, for instance, May 10th, these "cockles," or hard-backs, as they are called, came upon us like an army. They are a little black beetle about an inch long, with two pairs of wings, or, more strictly, one pair of wings and a hard, horny pair of wing sheaths over them; they have six legs and pretty strong claws, that enables them to cling firmly to whatever they alight on. They are very similar to the "blackjack" found in some of the poorer houses at home. As I enter the pulpit they come. Around the lamps they are flying in hundreds; they drop on my hymn-book as I read out the hymn; my pulpit-cushion is covered with them. I sweep them all off, and open the Bible; they are crawling over its pages; I pull half a dozen out of my hair; I shake them off my gown. I say, "Brethren, let us pray." I close my eyes; one is sticking its claws into my neck. I feel as if I could scream. I open my mouth—"Oh Lord!" they have got in between my teeth! *Perseverando vinces.* And thus the service goes on. Half the lights are put out; a number of lamp-glasses are broken; and on the floors, and on the seats, on the cushions and on the people, thousands upon thousands of hard-backs are lying and crawling. As soon as you get into the house you find them there; it is only when you get into your bedroom, where doors and windows have been closed and no lights burning, that you can get free from them. And what a relief it is!

The remarkable thing is, that though millions of these creatures must be left in the houses and on the floors at night, when the morning comes not one of them is to be seen—save, of course, those that you killed. The rest—

> "Did fold their tents like the Arabs,
> And as silently steal away."

One of the pleasing things about our worship here is the singing. It strikes the keynote. It is grand congregational singing. Every one takes his part. There is the soprano, the tenor, the alto, the bass. In addition to an organ we have a precentor, who leads with the cornet. And at our special musical services it is not uncommon to have several violins, a bass fiddle, and a number of brass instruments. You cannot be amongst this people long without finding it out that they are essentially a musical people. They play well on the piano, the violin, the cornet, the organ, and even the accordion and the tin whistle. The old banjo has its place at their social gatherings, and it is quite amusing to see them march round in a large schoolroom to the strains of—

> "Roll, Jordan, roll;
> Roll, Jordan, roll;
> I wants to go to heaven when I die
> To hear old Jordan roll."

Religion has put music into the soul of the benighted African. It is the love of God that makes people sing. The coolies from India, who are mostly Mohammedans and Hindoos, cannot sing. I have heard them humming in a low, melancholy monotone, that ends with a tremulous drawn-out note like the bleating of a sheep. And that seems the only music that their faith inspires.

But the Christian religion awakens harmonies that are infinite, and akin to the music of the spheres. The old slave-masters were often struck with the fact that as soon as the negro was converted he began to sing. He sang as he went to his work in the field, he sang in his night of sorrow and pain, just as the apostles did before him. "And at *midnight* Paul and Silas prayed and sang praises unto God, and the prisoners heard them." Would that the prisoners of to-day, those held in

IN A TROPICAL CHURCH

the bondage of superstition and error, might hear us sing, and be led to the knowledge of God!

But how about the knowledge of the Bible and religious truth? Are they not far behind in these things? In some respects, yes; and in others, no. The black people as yet have only had one book, and that book has been the Bible. To them it is full of marvellous history, incident, and story. It has spoken to them as no other book could. To them it is indeed a revelation from God. Before the missionaries came all was dark. They had never heard of a life beyond. As slaves, their hopes were earthbound. The grave was the limit of their horizon. What was there to live for? They were only valued as cattle upon the estate. "Nigger ain't got any soul," was the postulate laid down by their masters. They must eat and work and sleep to the sound of the task-masters' whips. But when the Bible was opened to them they heard of "One whose ear is ever open to the cry of the oppressed," and a new life began to pulsate through their being. The deliverance of Israel from Egypt's dark bondage, the overthrow of the mighty oppressor in the Red Sea, struck a chord in their hearts that brought tears to their eyes. Look at that old African poring over the letters of the alphabet that he might be able to read "de raal Word ob de Lord" for himself. This was an evidence of the intense hunger of his soul. The people here say "Hunger mak' tigah cross wattah"—water. So the hunger of these negroes made them steal away from their huts at night, and brave the threatened lash, to hear the good stranger tell them of the love of God in Christ Jesus.

> "Steal away! Steal away!
> Steal away home to Jesus.
> Steal away! Steal away home,
> I ain't got long to stay here."

So far the Bible has been the one book of the poor people. They have read it, and still read it with avidity. A change, however, is coming over the younger generation, and a change for the worse. Increase of knowledge means increase of peril. Inquiry lets in doubt. They must be fitted to meet the new foes that will come upon them.

In the knowledge of the letter of the Bible our people here will compare favourably with the people at home. But then we must never forget that the eye only sees what it brings with it the power of seeing. To Peter Bell—

> "A primrose on the river's brim
> A yellow primrose was to him,
> And it was nothing more."

IN A TROPICAL CHURCH

But to a botanist it is a beautiful specimen of a certain floral order, made up of stem, of sepals, of petals, of stamens and anthers. And to a poet it is a beautiful expression of a Divine feeling; it is the latest embodiment or incarnation of the soul of all beauty. Wordsworth says—

> "To me the meanest flower that blooms can give
> Thoughts that do often lie too deep for tears."

Our reading of the Bible is not equal. One sees only a simple story, another a detached truth, whilst a third sees in the same sentence a whole philosophy or a complete system of ethics. Only so much do we know as we have lived. And—

> "We live in thoughts, not breaths;
> In feelings, not in figures on a dial.
> He lives most, who thinks most,
> Feels the noblest, acts the best."

In the knowledge of the "letter" the black people here are well on, but in that deeper spiritual knowledge, in that grasp of "*the Faith*," which is the name for the beliefs which form the heart of the Christian religion, they have still very much to learn.

Another thing that lends interest to a Church out here is the different races that are often found worshipping together. At home your congregation is all of one colour. Here we have men and women of nearly all colours. In one pew you will find a white man and next to him a black woman or child. Then you will find those that are neither black nor white, but a mixture of the two. And of these you find all shades from cream colour to a dark brown. Then you will have a Chinaman and an East Indian, and sometimes a pew full of Indians from the upper reaches of the river. These will come in dressed only in a pair of blue cotton pants and a shirt. Now all these different races are the children of the great Father in heaven, and they come and kneel before the Lord the Maker of us all. To find a word for each the preacher must be both simple and profound. He must have sympathies that go low enough to take in the poorest and the worst, and he must have a heart broad and comprehensive as the glorious gospel he is called to preach.

A tropical church is not so strictly limited as the churches at home to the Sunday services. During the week days it is often brought into requisition. A musical service on the Monday night is by no means an uncommon thing. Then with cornet and trumpet and organ we praise the Lord. A conference on the different methods of Christian work sometimes takes the place of a

IN A TROPICAL CHURCH

Wednesday evening service. Then on a Tuesday afternoon the candidates meet together in the church. Baptisms during the day are sometimes taken there. And the names chosen are occasionally very amusing. One black man brought his child, and when the minister asked its name, he said, "Seriatim ad Valorem." On another occasion the parson said, "What is the name of the child?" the man said "Ax parson." The minister looked at him and said, " I don't understand you." " Well, parson," said the man, "my mind gie' me to go troo' de New Testament. I have had four boys; one was called Matthew, another Mark, another Luke, and another John; and this is 'Acts,' parson."

"Nannie Bellona," and "Queen Elizabeth," and "Prince Albert," and "John Pantaloon," and "Frank Locust" are names that grace our baptismal register. Another negro, whose child I christened, was called "Whiskey Emmanuel."

But one of the most interesting services is a wedding. It is not uncommon to have three or four hundred people present at this important ceremony. The ladies' dresses are superb. Green and yellow and pink and blue; all the bridesmaids, as a rule (and there are generally seven or eight), are dressed alike. The bride, with a floral wreath round her head, is dressed in white, with a train about four yards long. Not being able to sound the "*th*," they often make some ludicrous mistakes. Instead of saying, "Until death us do part," they say, "Until '*debt*' us do part"; and "hereby I give thee my 'trot'" for troth.

A story is told of a minister whose groom was about to be married. Being accustomed to touch his hat when his master spoke to him, he did the same thing as he stood before the altar repeating the marriage service. At last the minister, bending down to him, said, "Never mind touching your hat, but say, after me." Then, he said, "Wilt thou have this woman to be thy lawful wedded wife?" Up went his hand to his head, and he exclaimed, "After you, sir." This was too much for the minister's gravity, and the whole assembly laughed outright.

Funerals, which are sad events anywhere, are especially sad out here; for no sooner does a person die than he is to be buried. Decomposition sets in so rapidly that it is necessary to bury the dead within twenty-four hours.

A man will sometimes be alive at seven in the morning and lying in his grave before six in the evening. To us Europeans this at first seems a shocking thing. You left your friend last night apparently well; you get a note about twelve o'clock asking you to his funeral at five. On going up the river once we got to Coomacka. A poor black woman was getting into the little boat to take her to her home. She asked, " How is John ? " meaning her husband. The reply was, " We buried him yesterday." She threw up her hands with a scream and fell like a log of wood into the bottom of the boat. This was the first she had heard of it, and she had only been away four days. When she left for town he was hearty and well. Ah! friends, you know not how our hearts are often cut and bruised by these sad and sudden events. Out here more than anywhere do we need to remember the Master's words, " Watch ye, for ye know not in what hour your Lord doth come."

IX

PARSON AND GORGONZAMBE

EARLY one day an old African came to my door, and he said, "Morning, my massa. How you do, Gorgonzambe?" "I am well, thank you," I replied; "but you speak to me in an unknown tongue. What do you mean by calling me Gorgonzambe?" "My massa," he said, "me sal tell you. In Africa de medicine man am de doctah for a' we body, but you am de doctah for a' we soul; and de African name for de minister am Gorgonzambe, which mean God-doctor. When de soul am sick you mus' gib us medicine. My soul am too sick, dis heart too bad." I need not say that I pointed him to the Great Physician, who alone can heal the maladies of the soul.

This idea of God-doctor is evidently a very old one, and the Africans of to-day have most likely had it handed down to them from the Africans who dwelt in Egypt a long, long time ago. For Diodorus tells us that on the front of the first public library in Egypt was a memorable inscription with these words: "The Medicine of the Mind."

The black people recognise, perhaps more than our people at home, distinctly psychological diseases. For instance, a woman will come to me and complain of the bad treatment she suffers from some neighbour or friend or husband. In answer to my question, "What have you done to provoke him?" she replies "Me neber do not'ing. He hab a *bad mind* for me." "Was it always so?" I ask. "No, parson. One time he so nice and good—now me no able fo' please him." We have a similar thing in the case of Saul. *He* had a bad mind towards David and sought to kill him. It is spoken of in the Bible as an "evil spirit," and what is an evil spirit but a bad mind? A wife here, who finds that her husband's mind towards her has changed, will have resort to an "Obeah-man," that is, a kind of "witch doctor" who professes by means of herbs and other mysterious arts to be able to exert a charm over the person of any one, and thus change their heart or their disposition. I need hardly say that this superstition is dying out as the light of Christianity advances.

Not the Obeah-man, but Gorgonzambe, if he be real and true, can give effectual help in such cases. We read in the Word of God that "the preparation (*i.e.*, the disposings) of the heart in man, and the answer of the tongue, cometh from the Lord" (Prov. xvi. 1). That is, the disposings of men's hearts towards us or against us, towards what is good, holy, or divine, are from the Lord. When people have a "bad mind to us" we ought first of all to examine ourselves, and see if by our ways or our words we have given cause for it, and then, secondly, we ought to make it a matter of prayer to Almighty God, that He will change their hearts and make them well disposed towards us. "When a man's ways please the Lord, He maketh even his enemies to be at peace with him."

Our people here have also another expression which shows how much they are influenced by "soul dispositions." "Why were you not at the social gathering last night, Susie?" "Well, parson," is the reply, "mi mind no gi'e me." Or I say to another, "You should have gone to Georgetown yesterday. Why did you not go?" The answer is, "My mind gi'e me not fo' go." And who can say she was wrong? At some time or other we have all had our presentiment of coming good or evil. Sensitive souls, like a barometer, can often foretell the approach of a storm. It is wise to be guided by the voice within. The inmost is often the highest. The soul's emphasis is invariably right, and especially after solemn, earnest prayer.

Gorgonzambe, or the God-doctor, out here has a great and high calling. He is looked up to as one who can alone help in the most solemn crises of life. The doctor can prescribe for the body, but he cannot prescribe for the soul. Now we do not believe, as Carlyle says many people do, that "Soul is synonymous with stomach." We hold as Sir William Hamilton puts it, that "Man is not an organism, he is an intelligence, served by organs." Man *has* a body, but he *is* a soul. The most important thing about any man is this same soul. The soul does not live for the body, but the body for the soul. The house exists for the sake of the man that dwells in it, and not the man for the sake of the house. Though this earthly house of our tabernacle be dissolved, *i.e.*, disunited and resolved into its original elements, we have a building of God, *i.e.*, another house, "not made with hands, eternal in the heavens." One day I was called in to see a poor black girl who had been taken ill. She had strayed from the fold and was one of God's lost sheep. There she lay on a little bed on the floor. I had to communicate to her the sad message that her days and even hours on earth were numbered. The doctor had just been, and said he could do nothing; the case was hopeless. When I told her she turned her eyes full upon me for a moment, and then throwing up her arms, with a scream she cried, "Oh, what is to become of my poor soul!"

Gorgonzambe must enter softly into the chamber of sickness, he must kneel beside the bed in the solemn hour of death; he must speak words that have healing in them; there must go out of him virtue, *i.e.*, strength, power, that by it weak ones may rise up and stand upon their own feet, and even take up their palliasse and walk.

The variety and extent of Gorgonzambe's work is such that many of our ministers at home have no idea of. They (the people) come to him for counsel in all their distresses, and they come from all parts of the country. At home the minister's house is usually a quiet place; out here it is a place of activity and constant callers. In order to attend to the many cases that come for Gorgonzambe's aid I had to put on the door outside the following notice: "Hours of consultation 9 to 11 and 3 to 4." The little study became a kind of spiritual surgery. Sometimes there are as many as twenty people under the house, waiting for their turn to come in. To enter into each case sympathetically and give the counsel and help needed is a drain upon both brain and heart. This has gone on sometimes till twelve o'clock—breakfast cold upon the table, still they come, till one o'clock and even two. Then "tired nature" would hold out no longer, and orders are given to close the door— "Gorgonzambe can not see any more to-day."

But you say, "Where do they come from?" and "What do they come about?" One or two extracts from my notebook may answer these questions best:

December 6th. A poor old lady came with trembling and tears—she had not eaten food that morning—begging massa to get her a little help from the almshouse. She is over seventy and nearly blind. The desired help is given, and one poor soul is thus lightened of its burden.

A young black man called to "tell me goodbye." He is going into the bush to bleed ballata. This needs a word of explanation. Ballata is the milk or sap of the bullet tree; when the bark of the tree is cut it runs out. This they catch in a calabash. When exposed to the sun it hardens into a kind of gutta-percha, and is used for many things at home. Indeed, it is a valuable article of export.

Many of our black men are thus engaged in "ballata bleeding." They go away into the interior of the forest, carrying their provisions with them, and are often away for four or six or eight months. "Well, John," I said, "where are you going this time?" "Into the forest beyond the Corentyne," he replied. "Have you been there before?" "Yes, parson." "Had you any adventures?" Then he begins to tell me how one day they were all startled with the cry of the bush hogs; every man ran up a tree, quick; on the hogs come, there are over a hundred of them. They shoot. "Bush hog no able fo' climb tree. For the next week we have plenty good food to eat."

"How do you live?" I said. "We first of all put up a Benaab, near to where we are going to work, then we swing our hammocks under it, four or six of us together. When we knock off, just before dark, we gather sticks and light a fire. Dog keeps watch for us through the night."

"You are going away," said Gorgonzambe. "You may not be back for six months, you may never come back at all, for there are many dangers in this forest life. But remember, our Father in heaven is King of the forest. You can never get out of His sight. As the first man heard the voice of the

Lord God walking in the garden (Gen. iii. 8), so may you. Keep the Lord's day sacred in the forest. You can get together and sing; one of you can read a portion of Scripture, and another lead in prayer. And remember we in this sanctuary always pray for you. Be cheerful, be industrious, be agreeable one with another. Fear God, and know no other fear." Then giving him a few little tracts, and a few portions of Scripture, Gorgonzambe commended him and his to God in prayer. As soon as he has gone, in step three Indians from the interior. They are from Arowyma. Much sickness just now among the Indians. Two or three belonging to the Mission have just died. They want me to send a petition for them to the Governor for a box of medicines—pills, plasters, ointments, tinctures, &c., and plenty of quinine and oil, " Ready Relief," chlorodyne, &c. Gorgonzambe promises to attend to this matter at once. He then counsels them to meet often for prayer, to be good and faithful followers of Christ, and to prepare for the minister's next visit. Giving them a little money for their passage back, they are sent on their way rejoicing.

Another now enters. "Well Mrs. S——?" She is crying bitterly. Around her are five little children, one in her arms, the others clinging to her dress. "What is the matter?" Her husband is ill at Lichfield, *i.e.*, about twenty miles away. He had fallen from a building, and she had heard he was "bad nuff," that is, *in extremis*. How could she get to see him? There was only one way, and that was to cross the river in a boat and then go by the coach. This would cost two dollars, or even more. She had not even a "bitt." Gorgonzambe gave her the money, planned out for her the journey, arranged for the wife to bring her husband back and get him into the town hospital. This was done. Alas! the poor woman died a few months after. The struggle for her children, together with her anxiety, was too much for her. The husband still lives.

Mr. B. comes in, and asks Gorgonzambe to give him a testimonial. He has been out of work for months, knows not what to do, wife and children are famishing. He believes he can get this place if Gorgonzambe will only speak for him.

Mr. K. is summoned to appear at Court. The Commissary has seized his boat. He accuses him of cutting wood on the Crown lands. Will Gorgonzambe come and help him. After inquiring thoroughly into the whole case, Mr. K. is defended in Court, and the man is, after a patient hearing and investigation, dismissed.

Three men now come from away up beyond Brunswick. They want Gorgonzambe to petition the Government for a grant of land for them. This is done. They ultimately get three hundred acres of an abandoned estate, paying for it in three annual instalments.

A widow next comes in, young and blooming. She wants to marry again, but some say she must go to the Public Buildings and get an "Act of Verweezing." This will cost five or six or even ten dollars, according to the knowledge or want of knowledge of the person who applies. She wants Gorgonzambe's advice.

And thus the story goes on. Each new day brings its fresh batch of cases. All the rivers run into the sea, yet the sea is not full, but it soon would be if there were not an outlet for its waters, by way of evaporation towards heaven. So Gorgonzambe's heart would be too full, but he has learned to carry them to the throne of grace and lay the burdens of his people there.

The minister out here is called "parson," and the usual address is "Morning, parson," "How you do, parson?" And often when some of the females get into a quarrel and lift up their voices in the street, obeying the prophetic commands,

"Cry aloud, spare not, lift up thy voice with strength," there has been heard the quiet voice of some neighbour, "Hi! parson's coming!" Then the combatants have retreated for a time, smothering their wrath, but only to burst out again as soon as the parson has gone. I was very much struck one day in September with the saying of a good old black African woman. My wife happened in the midst of conversation about the dry weather to say "she feared the vat would be empty before the dry season was over." "No, no, missie, never fear, for *parson's vat never run dry.*" I thought that is perfectly true. There may not be much in it, but many a poor woman in her sorrow and distress, and many a poor parson in his time of need has found that the barrel of meal wasted not, and the cruse of oil did not fail.

The parson's vat of kindliness never runs dry. Hardly a day passes but many come to draw upon it. The poor, the distressed, the helpless, the crushed, when they know not what to do or where to turn, are sure of a kindly word and a helpful hand from the parson. "My husband is sick and dying, parson; will you come and see him?" Kindly inquiries are made and sympathetic words spoken, and soon the parson stands in the sick room, between the living and the dying, to speak

PARSON AND GORGONZAMBE

in gentle tones of Him who is the resurrection and the life.

Hardly has the footsteps of one visitor died away ere another unfortunate stands almost speechless pleading for pity and help. It is twelve o'clock, the visitor comes from the country, she has walked six miles in the broiling sun. "Nothing to eat, massa, for a me-self and picknies, ain't broke bread dis mornin'." A "bitt" put into the hand and directions to go into the kitchen to the cook, gives new life to the poor body, and she starts out hopefully looking for better days.

Another wants parson to make some villagers agree to dig out their trenches, and to help them to put in a new koker. Then comes another with a wicked boy whom the police have summoned. Will the parson please go and intercede for him. And thus twenty, thirty and forty in a day come to draw out of this vat of kindliness possessed by the parson. Sometimes there is not as much in the vat as at other times, but still it is mainly true, as the old black woman said, "*Parson's vat never runs dry.*"

Parson's vat from which he gets his sermons never runs dry. I don't say that he is never dry, but the source from which he draws his sermons is never dry. Sermons, like salt fish, are sometimes good and sometimes bad. Even parsons cannot always give you the best. No clock can strike twelve every time, not if its striking parts are right. People must be content sometimes to take milk instead of strong meat. When we consider what the parson has to do, how he has to produce his three sermons every week, and stand up before the same congregation year after year, besides his candidates' class, his Bible class, his lay preachers' class, his young people's classes, and in addition conducting services two or three times every week at various out stations, giving addresses and lectures, and doing a host of other things besides, it is a wonder how he gets through his work at all. Don't grumble if the sermon has not quite pleased you. Remember as father Taylor used to say, " Poor preachers are like camels, bearing precious spices and often feeding on bitter herbs." One of Charles II.'s chaplains was not liked as a preacher by the king, because he did not spare the king's vices. When told of it he said, "*If the King 'll mend I'll mend.*" That's the bargain parson will make with the people. " If you'll mend I'll mend." It's bad hearers that make bad speakers.

Monday morning is a restful morning to parson.

He feels so much *lighter*, as we all know he must do, after the *delivery* of such *weighty* discourses the day before. But as the week goes on he becomes anxious. When it gets towards the end he becomes positively uneasy. See him walking about in the study there, now looking up, now down, now lost in a maze of thought. He sits sometimes for hours, like a fisherman waiting for a nibble. He becomes as quiet as a hen that wants to lay. If a visitor comes to the door, Missie says, " I would not disturb him for anything, the results might be disastrous—an egg without a shell, or an untimely birth, or for that day no intellectual birth at all." Macaulay, writing to a friend, said, " Whatever I write, I must at present spin, like a spider, out of my own entrails." It is so with the true parson.

His sermons must come out of himself, they must be a part of his own mind and heart, and soul experience. Only that which we have felt and seen can we with confidence tell. Each Sabbath he must have his story ready, and this for ten, twenty, and thirty years. Surely he must feel sometimes that he has said all that he can say, that he has exhausted the book, having gone from Genesis to Revelation. What if some Friday or Saturday when he sits down to write, he should find that the vat has run dry. No; he begins to pump, as usual, and sure enough water, bright, fresh, sparkling as of yore, begins to flow. You are right, dark skinned prophetess, "*Parson's vat never run dry.*" And why? Because the heart of man is boundless, the soul of man is infinite. As Longfellow says:

> " The land of song, *within thee lies*,
>   Watered by living springs,
>
> . . . .
>
> *Look then into thy heart and write,*
>   *Yea, into life's deep stream.*
> All forms of sorrow and delight,
> All solemn voices of the night,
> That can soothe thee or affright,
>   Be these henceforth thy theme."

Parson's vat—namely the Bible, never runs dry.

That's the only new book in the world. It's the *one* book that is always fresh. You may let down your pitcher into it a thousand times, it is still as full as ever. Yea, the more you take from it the more there is to take. As an Englishman said, it is like a big round of roast beef, " you may cut and come again." It is a fountain fed from an unseen source, a river that springs from under the throne of God. To its living streams, the thirsty from all lands may come. Let us ever be thankful for *this vat*, and that *it* never runs dry. To it the parson comes day by day with his empty pitcher, and the secret of his own vat never running dry is that he has free access to this. Come ye thirsty, poor, and needy, and in your time of greatest distress remember what the poor old black woman said—"*Parson's vat never run dry.*"

A PARSON'S WORRIES

A parson sat in his study alone,
 Vainly striving to think,
But the people kept coming, one by one,
 Of his pity and counsel to drink.

First came one with a woe-begone face,
 Looking so dismal and down,
That the parson could hardly suppress a smile
 As his face relaxed from a frown.

"Well, my good man, and what is it for you?"
 " Ow' pa'sson me wife run away.
She hab lef' me with ten little picknies to keep,
 And me min' no gi'e me de way."

Well, Gabriel, man, you must fetch her back,—
 Take the steamer down, in the morn,
And here is a dollar to help you along,"
 Said he, with a hand-shake warm.

Then in comes a sprightly young negress,
 With face beaming over with joy :
"Mornin' passon !   Me want you to publish me banns,
 Me Quashee too bashful a boy."

Then in comes another—" Me wife be too sick,
   De fever and pains be too bad,
Please passon a paper to doctor fo' her?
   To look at she, make me too sad."

Then the fourth walks in with his black feet bare,
   And a bundle of deeds in his arm,
He wants to lay claim to some acres of land
   On which to establish a farm.

"You see, 'Sah,' me moder hab only one chile,
   And dat am me own own self.
Last week she did dead, and lef' me alone,
   And me fader lef' me dis wealth."

And so after questions and answers enough,
   The parson asks in despair,
" How long has you father been dead, my good man?"
   The answer comes, "Jus' seventeen year."

After patient inquiry and search had been made
   The parson discovered it all,
The land had been sold some twelve years ago,
   And this man had no claim at all.

Such are some of the troubles that come
   To parsons who work in these climes:
They need to be lawyers and doctors as well,
   Besides making their sermons betimes.

The people regard him as Fader and Frien',
   They come to him every day,
Each with his story and trouble and grief,
   For parson to help drive away.

                              L. E. C.

X

THE OLD AFRICANS OF GUIANA

WE must now turn aside a little in order to give some account of the people of this land. In doing so we have to remember that we are not dealing with one race, but many. Here we have black men from Africa, red men from India, yellow men from China, and white men from Europe. These all have their peculiarities of race as well as complexion. Their ways of thinking and looking at things, their manners and customs, their habits, their dress are all more or less tinged by their historic antecedents. For we are all what the past has made us. If we have a picture that we want to be seen, we put it in the best light that we can. Shall we do less for our fellow-men? They are here, suffering, working, dying:

" Toiling, rejoicing, sorrowing,
Onward through life we go."

Let us look at them with that charity which covers a multitude of sins.

Most of the people of this colony are *black*. If they are not Africans, they are the descendants of Africans. It is fashionable in some quarters to decry the black people. " They are lazy, they are improvident, they are dishonest, they are worthless," I have often heard it said. But those who say so, forget the sins which lie at their own door, and speak from a prejudiced, rather than a large-hearted philosophic point of view.

In judging the poor African we should not forget his origin and his past history, and the conditions under which he was brought to this country. The origin of the black man, like that of the white man, is sufficiently far back to admit of uncertainty and reasonable doubt. What colour was the first man? A smart negro replied, " Black, sir." " How, then, do you account for the white man?" "This way, sir. The first man had two sons. One was very good, the other very bad. The bad one being 'bex' rose up, and with a club felled his brother to the ground. Then the Lord came and said, ' Cain, where be Abel, thy brother?' Cain trembled when the Lord asked him this question, and turned PALE. The *pale* men are his descendants." We might ask the same question of a coolie, and he might tell us that the first man was "red," like himself. For does not the Bible say he was called "Adam," which means red or ruddy. My friend, the physiologist, explains the blackness of the sons of Africa by saying, "It is all owing to a little *black pigment* under the skin." But who put the black pigment there, and whence came it? Is it not reasonable to suppose that the colour of the skin, like many other differences, is simply the effect of country and climate. These acting through generations and for thousands of years have produced that "black pigment," and coloured the skin. In all other respects the African is a type of the *genus homo*. We might take up the language of Shylock and say, "Hath not an African eyes? Hath not an African hands, organs, dimensions, senses, affections, passions? Is he not fed with the same food, hurt with the same weapons, subject to the same diseases, healed by the same means, warmed and cooled by the same winter and summer? If you prick them do they not bleed? If you tickle them do they not laugh? If you poison them do they not die? And if you wrong them will they not be revenged?" And a writer in the inspired volume, who lived in days when men were held in bondage, taking a wide and philosophic view of men, says, " God hath made of one blood all nations of men for to dwell on all the face of the earth, and hath determined the times before appointed, and the bounds of their habitation ' (Acts xvii. 26). The introduction of the negro into this country was not of a kind fitted to give him a fair start in the race of life. He was torn from his homeland, loaded with heavy chains and placed in the hold of the ship. During his passage he was treated with a coarse brutality that would not be allowed now even in the transport of cattle. Landed on these shores he was regarded only as a beast of burden. Companies were formed to buy and use him as a species of cattle. Among the nations of the earth he was regarded as the child of ignominy and scorn. He was a helpless victim in the hands of hardened and cruel task-masters. A man more sinned against than sinning. The cruelties of the slave life, and the hardships endured, we all know something of, but the full sufferings of these poor wronged negroes will never be known till the great Books are opened. The Rev. John Wray, in his diary penned in this Berbice of ours in 1817, says, " On Easter Tuesday morning we saw two white men with the manager and a strange boat at the wharf; afterwards, while teaching some children, a white man in a blue jacket, and with a stick in his hand, driving a negro, passed the window, but they were too far off to hear what was said. Soon drivers came, fixed some stakes in the ground, then brought the negro, stretched him all naked on the ground, and tied his hands and feet to the stakes. Standing one on each side they began to flog him with their cart whips. About seventy lashes had been given, when Mrs. Wray, who had been looking out of another window, called to the white men for God's sake to have mercy on the sufferer; they, however, went on till the poor fellow had received one hundred."

Anxious to know what the man had done to deserve all this, Mr. Wray was told it was for impertinence to a magistrate, himself a slave-holder, who had come to visit the provision grounds. It seems that one of this visitor's slaves had stolen 5s. 6d. from this negro on the Sandvoort Estate, who hearing that the thief's master was in the manager's house, came and pressed his request that the money should be refunded. The magistrate was angry and told him to go.

The negro said: "Massa, so long as me poor negro, massa no want for give me right; massa no tell me if the negro shall pay me or no."

Magistrate. If you do not go I will flog you.

Negro. If we had come on massa's plantation

and tieved, massa would come and flog all we, and our massa would make us pay the negro what we tieved from him.

Magistrate strikes him on the head with a stick.

Negro. Me come to beg massa for me right, and massa beat me upon the top of my right.

Magistrate drives him forth, and becoming judge, jury, and virtual executioner in his own cause, inflicts the punishment narrated. ("Wray's Life," p. 141).

One hundred lashes for demanding his right, and that by a man who was supposed to be a pillar of justice! The same year—September 3rd —he, Mr. Smith, writes: "Saw some niggers working in irons, and one whose skin was entirely cut off his back with the whip. Oh, slavery! thou offspring of the devil, when wilt thou cease to exist? Never, I think, was my sense of vision more disgusted with the degradations of the human species or my feelings more keenly touched. Hark! I pause in the midst of this —a terrible thunderstorm—to count the lashes on the naked slave. This is the first thing on the Monday morning (August 8, 1818). When the flogging was over, Mrs. S. called out to me, 'Did you count those lashes?' 'Yes.' 'How many did you reckon?' I said 141. I then asked her if she had counted them. She said, 'Yes ; I counted 140'" (p. 355).

This cruelty was inflicted upon women as well as upon men. And one case we know of where a negress who was *enceinte*, was stripped and laid upon the ground, and most barbarously flogged. There are some writers who try to minimise the evils and horrors of slavery. But when they have whitewashed it over with all the fine phrases that they are capable of, its lurid blackness still remains. But flogging alone was not the only degradation. There was the slave market and the auction sale. *There* might be seen the lordly planter, the usurious speculator, the insatiate sensualist, and even the timid female and the pampered child. They are gathered in groups around the dark children of Africa, who, with anxious hearts and downcast eyes, await the results. A purchaser would approach and examine the qualities of the negro he was about to buy. The scanty covering of the slave threw but a sleight veil over the figure and form. The limb was carefully examined and tested, the surface of the body scrutinised for the detection of any morbid condition of the skin, the mouth was inspected, the functions of walking, running, and lifting were practised at the desire of the party about to make an offer. Delicacy, pity, generosity, never interfered with the mercenary considerations which regulated these proceedings ("Dalton," i. 165).

"Pincard" gives an account of one of these sales in 1796. "Just a hundred years ago," he says, "I saw what is here termed a prime cargo of three hundred men and women from the Gold Coast of Africa. The crowd was as great as at Coventry Fair, and amid the throng I observed many females, as well white as of colour, who, decked out in tinsel finery, had come to the mart to buy slaves for themselves, their masters, or keepers. Infants, too, were brought to point the lucky finger to a sable drudge for little self. The poor blacks were divided into three great lots, according to their value. Boys from eleven to fourteen were sold for six hundred or seven hundred florins. Women were sold for seven hundred or eight hundred florins, and men seven hundred to nine hundred florins. Amid this scene so repugnant to humanity a general sympathy was excited towards one particular family, whose appeals to the compassion of the multitude were not less powerful than their claims. This family consisted of a mother, three daughters, and a son. The mother, although the days of youth were past, was still a

SLAVES LANDING FROM THE SHIP.

good-looking woman. The children appeared to be from fourteen to twenty years of age. They were very like the mother, and still more resembled each other, being all of distinguished face and figure, and quite the handsomest negroes of the whole cargo. Their distress lest they should be separated and sold to different masters was so strongly depicted upon their countenances, and expressed in such lively and impressive appeals, that the whole crowd were led impulsively to commiserate their sufferings, and by general consent they were removed from the three great lots and placed in a corner separate by themselves. Observing their extreme agitation I was led particularly to notice their conduct, as influenced by the terror of being torn from each other. When any one approached their little group, or chanced to look toward them with the attentive eye of a purchaser, the children, in broken sobs, crouched to their tearful mother, who, in agonising impulse, instantly fell down before the spectator, bowed herself to the earth, and kissed his foot; then alternately clinging to his legs and pressing her children to her bosom, she fixed herself upon her knees, clasped her hands together, and in anguish cast up a look of humble petition which might have found its way even to the heart of a Caligula."

What became of them history knows not. Some of their descendants may be here amongst us to-day. But that families were torn from each other we know—wives torn from husbands, never to look upon each other's face again; children torn from parents, only to meet when the last trumpet sounds.

THE SLAVE-MOTHER'S FAREWELL

  Gone, gone,—sold and gone
  To the rice-swamp dank and lone.
Where the slave-whip ceaseless swings,
Where the noisome insect stings,
Where the fever demon strews
Poison with the falling dews,
Where the sickly sunbeams glare
Through the hot and misty air,—
  Gone, gone,—sold and gone,
  To the rice-swamp dank and lone,
  From Virginia's hills and waters,—
  Woe is me, my stolen daughters!

  Gone, gone,—sold and gone,
  To the rice-swamp dank and lone.
There no mother's eye is near them,
There no mother's ear can hear them;
Never, when the torturing lash
Seams their back with many a gash,
Shall a mother's kindness bless them,
Or a mother's arms caress them.

THE OLD AFRICANS OF GUIANA

>   Gone, gone,—sold and gone,
>   To the rice-swamp dank and lone,
>   From Virginia's hills and waters,—
>   Woe is me, my stolen daughters!
>
>   Gone, gone,—sold and gone,
>   To the rice-swamp dank and lone,—
>   Toiling through the weary day,
>   And at night the spoiler's prey.
>   Oh that they had earlier died,
>   Sleeping calmly, side by side,
>   Where the tyrant's power is o'er,
>   And the fetter galls no more!
>   Gone, gone,—sold and gone
>   To the rice-swamp dank and lone,
>   From Virginia's hills and waters,—
>   Woe is me, my stolen daughters!
>   WHITTIER.

About one hundred thousand slaves were in this colony at the beginning of this century. Their condition can be better imagined than described. Degraded to the condition of animals, they were driven out almost naked to the fields to work. The sound of the task-master's whip was ever in their ears. At night they were sent to their stables, like so many horses, to fit them for the next day's work. Morality there was none. Marriage was unknown amongst them. The lordly planter, having them at his own disposal, used them for the basest purposes. One and another he selected, as inclination prompted, for the his mother tongue. As he spoke he begged us to excuse him, for, said he, "I have to think first in the Bechuana language and then translate it into English." Speaking of his life there, and the love that still burnt in his breast for God's image in ebony, he said, "Oh, Africa! Africa! Would I were young again, how gladly would I give my life for thee, oh Africa."

Of David Livingstone and his travels through that land, of his heroic patience and endurance, of the influence which, like a track of light, has followed behind him, let his biographers speak. Africa has been opened out, its darkness is vanishing, and the down-trodden sons of Ham are being lifted up. Now contrast this with the other picture. A number of men have gone forth; they have formed themselves into companies. What for? To buy, to enslave, to use as a beast of burden, to crush every spark of manhood out of this same poor African. The one set of men seek to lift up the negro, to break his chains, to arrest his deteriorations, and place him among the nations of the earth as a man, a brother, and a son of God. The other by their methods and designs rivet afresh his chains, degrade him to the level of a beast, crush and blight his Godward instincts, degrade and destroy his manhood and his soul.

To which band, reader, would you rather belong? There are some who try to excuse the planters on the ground of the darkness of those days. But the light which Moffat and Wray had was as accessible to them. Then again, it is said they wanted labourers. What for? To enrich themselves and fill their own coffers. Exactly, the demon of avarice, the devil of selfishness was at the bottom of it all. To gratify *that*, they were prepared to trample on God's image, and violate every principle of justice and humanity. "Advocatus Diaboli" is the name of that man, whoever he may be, who seeks to justify the slave-holder or extenuate slavery. To the hundred thousand slaves in this colony "John Wray" came in 1807. He was the shepherd sent out to seek and save these lost sheep. He was a brave-hearted Yorkshireman, and nobly he toiled and suffered for the sake of the oppressed. The plantocracy and the plutocracy did all that they could for a time to hinder him in his work. But when God says, "Let there be light," no power in the world can keep it back. You might as well try to keep back the Atlantic tide with a broom. The day had dawned. The Christian missionary was the advance guard. The slaves heard of God, of Christ, of the soul, of salvation, of heaven. A new world opened to his view, a new life throbbed in his veins. He was still a slave, but he was free. The master might chain his body, but he could not chain his soul. For the first time these slaves were heard singing. Singing in the early morning, singing through the night.

> "Singing for Jesus glad hymns of devotion,
> Lifting the soul on her pinions of love,
> Dropping a word or a thought by the wayside,
> Telling of rest in the mansions above."

John Wray was *the first Christian minister* in British Guiana who opened his lips to show the way of salvation to the people then in slavery. Think of that, ye black people, and let his name be dear to you and your children. There were one or two other ministers—an Anglican, who was chaplain to the soldiers, and a Dutch, who ministered to the Dutch planters—but their churches and their gospel were for the whites only. The doors were barred against the negroes. For the planters held, as the *Royal Gazette* of that period (1808) said : " It is dangerous to make slaves Christians." Yes ; and so it is. Dangerous to the usurper of another's rights ; dangerous to the oppressor in his wrong doings ; dangerous to those who would traffic in flesh and blood and keep men's souls in darkness and in chains. We are not surprised, then, to find "an officer of the law" at the door of the church to keep the slaves away. In New Amsterdam there was an old Dutch church. It stands here still, but beautified and renovated, outside and inside, in its creed as well as in its conduct. Over its portals is a beautiful Latin inscription, "Solus Deo gloria"—which the people can't quite understand. One person translated it and called it "the solid glory" church. In front of that "solid glory" church in the old days a signboard was to be seen with the words: "*Negroes and dogs are not permitted to enter here!*" Dogs and negroes! Aye, and some of the dogs were better housed and fed than many of these poor people. But, thank God, even the "dogs eat of the crumbs which fall from the Master's table"—crumbs of mercy, crumbs of truth, crumbs of hope, crumbs of that "Bread of Life," which came down from heaven. They are eating of it to-day. And the old Dutch church throws its doors wide open to them, and atones for its past wrong by giving to all a hearty welcome.

But things have changed since then. And it is largely owing to the patient, consecrated toil of men like Wray, Davies, Elliot Smith, Ketley, Henderson, &c., &c., all of whom were sent out by the London Missionary Society.

The minister of this Lutheran Church to-day was trained by the London Missionary body, and is a descendant of that once hated race.

The gospel to the negro was a real message from heaven. It was a lighted candle in the dark chamber of his soul. He saw things which he had never seen before. The world became a different place to him. He had now something to live for. No threats and no scourging could make him give up his faith. He believed in his Bible, and he believed in prayer. A certain slave named "Gingo," who used to set the tunes in Bethel Chapel, was frequently employed by his master in what is called task-work, and on these occasions he was usually told, "Now, Gingo, when you have completed this you may go to pray." One day the planter said, "Gingo, I find the best way to get anything done quickly is to tell the negroes that they shall go to pray." The poor fellow replied, "*Me glad Massa know dat pray do all tings.*"

Mr. Wray, in his diary, 1812, says, "Mr. De la Court told me of a negro who, a few weeks before, had been severely flogged for preaching. The negroes had been teaching the catechism and praying, and some of the masters called this preaching. I had occasion to speak to some of the negroes on this matter. They replied that 'Buckra no know preach from pray; and when we pray, Buckra call it preaching.' Buckra means 'white man.' And so poor 'Sambo' got flogged for preaching when he was only praying. But that only made him pray the more. 'And the Lord said, I have surely seen the afflictions of my people which are in Egypt, and have heard their cry, by reason of their task-masters; for I know their sorrows and am come down to deliver them' (Exod. iii. 7)." The fiat had gone forth. Slavery was doomed. Already the advance guard were at work. Wray and Davies and Smith had entered into the land, and they were crying, "Prepare ye the way of the Lord, make His paths straight." They were teaching the slaves to read, and many an old negro might have been seen at night by the light of a dim candle spelling out some blessed text, and as he made out the words with difficulty, "God so loved the world," and "Come unto Me and rest," he would cry out in his joy, "Is dis de raal word ob de Lord? Bless de Lord, O my soul!" And many a "flogging" has been received for thus "reading" and teaching others to read and to pray. One poor slave woman came to parson Smith one day in great distress. "Oh my massa," she cried, "de rats eat all my book; it all gone, massa." Then, opening her kerchief, she showed the bits of paper—all that remained of her precious treasure. "Massa," she said, "de rats going ruin me; dey eat my kerchief, dey eat my salt fish, dey eat my plantain, dey take de cotton out ob my lamp. Me no mind all dis, but now"—and the tears rolled down her face—"dey hab eat my book. When me go look fo' my book me find it *so*, den me cry, and me go show massa what de rats hab done." Poor "Minky"! She and the rats and the massa have all alike gone. Worms have finished them all up, so far as the "bodies" are concerned. For nature and Revelation have said, "Then shall the dust return to the earth as it was, and the spirit shall return unto God who gave it" (Eccles. xii. 7). We are following on. The same trouble comes upon us. The rats are eating our Bibles. There is the rat of "indifference," the rat of "neglect," and the great cane rat of "unbelief." These and many others are eating away our best "Book"—and not only so, but they are destroying the very wick of our lamp—"the lamp of knowledge and of the fear of the Lord." "And the foolish said unto the wise, 'Give us of your oil, for OUR lamps are *gone out*.' The rats have ruined us."

XI

EMANCIPATION AND ITS RESULTS

ONE of the first acts of the Reform Parliament of 1832 was the Act of Emancipation. They who had just entered into a large measure of political liberty showed "what spirit they were of" by granting liberty to the slaves of the West Indies at a cost to the English people of twenty million pounds sterling. Never was money better spent. And yet it was a gross injustice. It was like paying a man for property to which he had no intrinsic right, and for which, according to the highest law of equity, he could establish no claim. To the glory of the English people let it be said that they struck off the chains that bound in perpetual slavery the poor negro. They stretched out a hand of sympathy to him in language which said, "Thou, too, art a man and a brother." The African is still grateful. He will never forget it. His heart still bounds with kindly thoughts of England. The great white nation is to him the "great massa." England they call home. It is the home of their freedom, the home of their religion, the home of all that is noblest and best in their life. The great Queen they call mother, and some of the old negresses who remember slave time will have it that the Queen is a black woman like themselves. May this kindly feeling never cease to exist, but may it deepen and extend until the black people become as great and as prosperous as the white race across the sea.

To understand the effect of the Act of Emancipation, which came into force on the 1st of August, 1834, we must look at the condition of the Africans here and some of the important events that preceded it.

In this colony there were about a hundred thousand slaves: the actual number on which compensation was claimed was 82,824. Besides these there were the whites, chiefly Europeans, masters and lords of all. They were the dominant class—the rulers, the judges, the soldiers, the landowners: they claimed everything. But they were comparatively few in number; in some parts not more than one in forty, and on many of the plantations not more than one in sixty. Some of the plantations had from five to six hundred slaves, all of whom were under the management of one white man, assisted by five or six white overseers. The responsibility of the whites was, therefore, very great. "From their hands," says a writer who lived in the colony about that time, "the hundreds of slaves under them must receive everything, as well their food, physic, and punishments, as their orders to work. And their example gives a powerful bias to the principles and the conduct of those whom they govern. On the plantation much more care and attention are bestowed upon the horses and cattle than upon the negroes, especially where there is no resident proprietor. Neither do the planters seem to regard the effects of their example upon the morals of the slaves; if they did, they would surely abstain from those barefaced indecencies so prevalent among them, or at least endeavour to conceal their gross immoralities from the vulgar gaze."

The result of "these indecencies" so prevalent among them, "was a mixed race, more or less white or black. Some of these were added to the slave gangs, and others were more privileged, and enjoyed a kind of semi-freedom. Then there were the free coloured people who formed a class by themselves. With the whites they had little connection, and they were too lofty to associate with the blacks."

The slaves are employed mostly in the cultivation of the ground. The plantation is their place of work. "At about six in the morning," says an old writer, "the ringing of a bell or the sound of a horn is the signal for them to turn out to work. No sooner is this signal made than the black drivers, loudly smacking their whips, visit the negro houses to turn out the reluctant inmates, much in the same manner as you would turn out a number of horses from a stable yard, now and then giving a lash or two to any that are tardy in their movements. Issuing from their kennels nearly naked, with their implements on their shoulders, they stay not to muster, but immediately proceed to the field, accompanied by the drivers and a white overseer. In the middle of the day they are allowed about an hour and a half for rest and refreshment. Soon after sunset (which is always within about fifteen minutes of six) they leave off work in the field, and each one having cut a bundle of grass for the master's horses, which serves instead of hay—an article not made in the West Indies—they bend their course homewards. They all carry the grass to a certain spot, forming a general muster, and there remain in the open air, often shivering with cold, till the cracking of the whip informs them they are to take it to the stable, which is generally about eight o'clock. If there be no other work to do, they may then go to their houses. I say 'If there be no other work,' for after toiling all day many of the slaves are frequently compelled to work nearly half the night, especially when they are making sugar, which is six months out of the twelve. Some are employed in grinding, some in boiling the juice, others in carrying away the cane trash, while another part of the gang is employed in carting or shipping sugar, rum, &c. Even the Sunday is not often given to them as a day of rest. 'Is it not better,' say the planters, 'to make them finish their work on a Sunday, than to be always punishing them? The Fourth Commandment says: "Six days shalt thou labour and do ALL thy work." It therefore follows, if ALL our work be not done in six days, we must finish it on the seventh.' Such reasoning only shows how easy it is for men to wrest the Scriptures to their own destruction."

In 1823 a rumour got abroad among the slaves that something good had come out for them from England. What it was they did not know, but some said the king and Parliament had made them free. A negro slave waiting upon the planters heard them discussing about it over their wine. The news spread like wildfire—"Freedom had come out from home." No official information had been given, and the slaves concluded that the Governor and their masters had combined to keep their freedom from them. This led to a rising of the slaves on plantation La Resouvenir on the east coast. Their design was to seize and put in the stocks all the white people on the estates, and then proceed to the town in a body to claim the freedom granted to them by the king.

It was in connection with this uprising that the Rev. John Smith was ruthlessly seized and cast into jail, on a charge of promoting discontent and rebellion, and being an accessory thereto. Before a court-martial of military men, whose prejudices against the missionary were only equalled by their incapacity to form a just judgment on such a case, he was, to their everlasting shame and disgrace, found guilty. Throughout the trial every effort was made by his unconstitutional judges to place him at a disadvantage ; and had there not been in the minds of these judges the most inveterate prejudices they would have seen that the evidence adduced could justify no other conclusion than a *full and honourable acquittal.*

Dr. Stephen Lushington, in the House of Commons, said : "No honest jury ever pronounced

"DE GREAT MASSA HAB MADE US FREE."

such a sentence as that which the court-martial at Demerara pronounced upon Mr. Smith; and it could have emanated from nothing but a virulent spirit of prejudice. *They knowingly and wilfully gave a false verdict.*"

The editor of the *New Times* in London said: "We have never in the whole course of our legal reading met with a sentence so utterly unsupported by the semblance of rational proof. Mr. Smith is found guilty of aiding and assisting in rebellion because a man whom he did not know to be even a reputed rebel came one day to his house, unexpected by him, stayed there a few minutes, and left it, without proof of a single word having passed between them."

Mr. Brougham, afterwards Lord Brougham, whom I had the pleasure of seeing once when I was a little boy at school, speaking in the House of Commons, said: "The precise offence of which Mr. Smith was declared to be guilty was termed '*misprision of treason.*' But the evidence given on the trial does not sustain this mitigated charge. And if it did, were this offence proved against him, it would not justify the sentence awarded. A man convicted of misprision cannot by law be hanged. The utmost vengeance of the law, according to the wildest dreams of the highest prerogative lawyer, could not amount to anything like a sanction of this. Such I assert the law to be; I defy any man to contradict my assertion that up to the present hour no English lawyer ever heard of misprision of treason being treated as a capital offence; and that it would be just as legal to hang a man for a common assault. But if it be said that the punishment of death was awarded for having aided the revolt, I say the court did not, could not, believe this; and I produce the conduct of the judges themselves to confirm what I assert. They were bold enough in trying and convicting and condemning the victim whom they had *lawlessly seized upon*, but they trembled to execute a sentence so prodigiously *illegal* and *unjust*.

"And this recommendation to mercy was the most remarkable feature in the conduct of this infamous court; for monstrous as the whole proceedings were, and horrid as the sentence was that closed them, there is nothing in the trial, from first to last, so astounding as this recommendation to mercy, coming from persons who affected to believe him guilty of such enormous crimes. If he was proved to have committed the offence of exciting the slaves to acts of bloodshed, if his judges believed him to have done what their sentence alleged against him, how unspeakably aggravated was his guilt compared with that of the poor, untutored slaves whom he had misled from their duty, under the pretext of teaching them religion! How justly might all the blood that was shed be laid upon his head! How fitly, if mercy was to prevail, might his deluded instruments be pardoned, and himself alone be singled out for vengeance, as the author of their crimes! Yet they are cut off in hundreds by the hands of justice, and he is deemed an object of compassion! Having declared that in their conscience and on their oaths his judges deemed him guilty of the worst of crimes, they all in one voice add that they also deem him deserving of mercy in respect of his guilt. Is it possible to draw any other inference from this marvellous recommendation than that they distrusted the sentence to which it was attached? When I see them, frightened by their own proceedings, starting back at the sight of what they had not scrupled to do, can I give them credit for any fear of doing injustice—*they who from the beginning to the end of their course had done nothing else?* Can I believe that they paused upon the consummation of their work from any motive but a dread of its consequences to themselves? a recollection tardy indeed, but appalling, that 'Whoso sheddeth man's blood, by man shall his blood be shed.' And not without reason, not without irrefragable reason, did they take the alarm; for, verily, if they had perpetrated the last act—if they had dared to take this INNOCENT man's life, one hair of whose head they durst not touch, they must THEMSELVES have died the death of MURDERERS."

Sixty years have passed away since those days, and many are the changes that have taken place. Nearly all the old Africans have gone to the place where the wicked cease from troubling and the weary are at rest. New generations have sprung up. Old customs have given place to new. There has been growth and rapid development. Larger ideas of life and greater intelligence are gradually bringing the native black people and the Creoles abreast of the times. Our educational system, though not perfect, is at least teaching the young people to read and write; and it is an interesting sight to go into one of our large schools filled with black and coloured children and watch them at their lessons. We have a large staff of native teachers, who on the whole are a credit to their country, and they work hard for the small salaries that are usually given. The work of the missionaries, of which the Rev. John Wray was the pioneer, has steadily gone on. Other churches have been established, and to-day the field is well occupied. We have churches and chapels in nearly every part of the land. In a certain superficial sense we may say we are nationally religious, for have we not a National Church—yea, churches—and a large number of official ecclesiastics? But whilst we are formally religious, we are yet far from it in reality. It is still possible for a nation to have many priests, and at the same time much paganism.

Ecclesiasticism and religion though conjoined are not the same thing. You may have a great deal of the former with very little of the latter; just as we may have a great deal of law and very little justice, and many physicians but few cures, so we may have many churches and not much religion. Religious people, strictly so, are good; ecclesiastics are often bad. Jesus Christ found His best friends among the peasants of Galilee and His bitterest foes amongst the ecclesiastics of Judæa. Ecclesiasticism crucified Christ, and it needs a Christ crucified to save ecclesiastics. The reason for all this is that religion has to do with the soul; ecclesiasticism has to do with the sacraments. The one is outward and formal, the other inward and spiritual. To give a history of ecclesiasticism is not to give a history of religion. It is too often a striking example of the want of religion. Churches have disgraced Christianity; Christianity has never disgraced Churches. The popular mind has failed to distinguish between these two, and even governments have thought that by establishing Churches they were establishing religion.

When Goethe was asked, "What is the best government?" he replied, "That which teaches us to govern ourselves." Yes, that is the lesson we all need to learn—to stand upon our own feet, to solve our own life problem, to work out our own destiny; this is the duty of every man. "Let your government commence in your own breast, and lay the foundation of it in the command of your own passions." But governments in these days must do nearly everything for us. Our Government in British Guiana is very paternal; it brings people into the colony by thousands to work for us, lest by sparsity of labourers wages should get up, and it is well known they are not by any means too high; it provides a fine staff of medical men, at an annual cost of $300,000, to to keep the people, or a portion of them, in health; and it pays a fine class of ecclesiastics to look after our souls. The people, therefore, ought to be both very healthy and very virtuous. As a matter of fact, they are neither. If the Government would first lighten the burden of taxation, and give material help in bringing labour and land together, and in all well digested schemes for the opening up of the country, better results would soon be seen.

Many of our people at home do not know that in this country we have not only an established Church, but established Churches. With a sublime indifference the Government makes its grant to Protestant and Romanist alike, to Scotch Presbyterians and English Episcopalians. It never asks the question, Which is true? or, Which is false? We might almost adopt the words of Gibbon, in his " Decline and Fall ": " The various modes of worship which prevailed in the Roman world were all considered by the people as equally true, by the philosopher as equally false, and by the magistrate as equally useful."

The cost of our ecclesiastical establishments is a hundred thousand dollars per annum. This is divided between the Anglican Church, the Scotch Church, the Roman Catholic Church, and—tell it not in Gath!—the Wesleyan Church. The only Church that takes its stand on the voluntary principle is the Congregational, or, as the native people here call it, the London Missionary. These churches, some forty in number, including mission stations, have nobly taken their stand as Free Churches in the land, and they have steadfastly refused all State aid. Their noble example and the soundness of their principles are like leaven, gradually leavening the whole lump, and the day is now within measurable distance when State Churchism in this land will be done away with—and the Free Churches will be able to do their work with reconsecrated energy amongst a free people.

XII

UP THE BERBICE RIVER

MONDAY, the 16th of March, was a very busy day for us. We had many callers that morning, and in addition to the usual work of a busy minister with over a thousand people to look after, we had to prepare for our journey of two hundred miles into the interior. Many little things will be necessary, for we are going far away from the haunts of civilisation. It is a return to those simple and primitive conditions of existence which prevailed in the Garden of Eden. The Indian aborigines are the children of the forest. Amid its majestic trees—its wallaba, its mora, its green heart, its purple heart, and its bullet tree, &c.—they wander according to their own sweet will. With cutlass and arrow and knife they hunt for their food, fetching the labba out of his hole and tracking the bush-hog and the deer. Such a life knows nothing of those refinements that give ease and comfort to the initiated. Its wants are few, and if a man's riches consist, not in the abundance of his possessions but in the fewness of his wants, then these aborigines are rich. Dispensing with all unnecessary commodities, the Indian lives a kind of untamed life amid the wilds of his native forest. The chirp of the insects, the croak of the frogs, the plaintive whistle of the monkeys, the shrill cry of the birds, is music enough for him. For his pictures he has the far-stretching, undulating savannah, the rich leafage of the forest, and the little creeks with their overhanging trees, giving such wondrous beauty of form and light and shade. He dispenses with chairs and tables and sofas. He needs no knives or forks or spoons; his fingers do duty for them. For cups and saucers and glasses he has a good substitute in the calabash which grows wild upon the trees. In fact the Indian has only two things, his hammock and his cooking pot. With these he can be as happy as a king. His hammock is his *vade mecum*. He carries that with him wherever he goes. The Indian's hammock is his chair, his table, his sofa, his bed. It is made, like most of the things he uses, out of the wood of the forest. When up amongst the

Arawacks we saw a Buckeen, or Indian woman, with one of these hammocks in process of construction. The beautiful palm tree called the Ita palm, in addition to many other useful qualities, possesses a strong fibre, which they draw out and twist into a thread; these threads are again twisted into a string, and these, by a simple hand-loom process, are worked into a strong, durable, network hammock. These hammocks are about eight feet long and seven feet wide, with a loop for a handle at each end. They will bear the heaviest of men, and last a long time. They are far preferable in these regions to beds. In the hammock you are suspended in mid-air, and so you escape those numerous insects and reptiles that crawl upon the floor. In the Benaab, where we stayed, it would have been simply impossible to sleep in a bed. The big red ants, called "cushi ants," were so numerous, and the beetles and the spiders and the lizards, that we should have been bitten and blistered from head to foot In addition to this you sometimes find yourself in a place where trees must be your bedposts and the tropical sky your covering, then a hammock becomes the traveller's indispensable. After a night's rest you have only to fold it up and "take up your bed and walk." But we must get back to our packing. Our boxes are nearly ready. We have got some tea and sugar and butter—the latter is in an air-tight tin, and runs like oil; also some Swiss milk, for there are no cows up there, and some tinned meats and some loaves of bread. These, after about ten days, get mouldy, and we can just break them with an axe, but put them in boiling water and they soon get soft. "Have you put the salt in?" I ask; for how can we live without salt? "Yes, massa, ebery ting dere," is the reply of the little black boy. I will see to the medicines myself, for I always like to have with me a few simple remedies in case of accident or unexpected attacks of fever. The quinine I must not forget, for some parts of the district—those where the swamps lie—are said to be very malarial, and the quinine is a splendid antidote. As soon as daylight dawns we are up, and by half-past six we are making our way to the river side. The boat is alongside, and having got our luggage in, we take our places and wait for the whistle.

The Berbice river is a fine stream. It is navigable for steamships of considerable size for upwards of two hundred miles. It is about two and a quarter miles broad at its mouth, near which the town of New Amsterdam stands. It abounds in sharks and alligators and other monsters of the

MATTED ROOTS OF COURIDA.

deep; and when sailing up the river it is wise to keep your hands well out of the water, as there is a fresh-water shark called the "homa" which has a special liking for fingers and toes. The windings of the river present to the careful observer a new picture at every turn. Sometimes you could fancy you were sailing on a lake: the waters are so placid, and the forest trees forming the embankment seem to close it in.

When you have passed the few villages and sugar estates which are at this end of the stream you find the banks all lined with massive trees, the rich foliage of nearly every shade dipping down to the water's edge. The trees are so knit together with prolific creepers, or "lianos," which entwine themselves among the branches and around the trunks, that they form an impenetrable thicket. This forest of trees extends all along both banks of the river. Its depth for the most part has not been explored. It runs "aback," as they say, far, far, far, that is for miles upon miles. But here and there as you sail along you find a little opening. The bush has been cut down, and a little hut appears; it is the dwelling-place of some African or coolie squatter. Behind the few trees stretches away as far as the eye can see the vast, untrodden savannah.

BRITISH GUIANA

It is now just turned six o'clock. "The shades of night are falling fast." By half-past six it will be quite dark. It is not considered safe to navigate the river in the dark, on account of stray logs that are sometimes floating down the stream, and then there is the danger of running into the banks or being caught by some branch of a tree. So having placed ourselves in the middle of the river, we cast anchor. It is a wise precaution to keep well clear of the banks of the river, for on either side are mosquitoes and sandflies. Snakes lie hidden in the long grass, and the mass of intertwining undergrowth is full of all kinds of stinging insects and creeping reptiles. Then there are ravenous beasts—tigers and tiger-cats, jaguars, crab-dogs, bush-hogs, and the bush-cow, besides many others of a less ravenous kind, but equally to be avoided.

One of the first things to be done, now that the boat is at anchor, is to find a place to hang one's hammock, for no sleeping place is provided here. You must just do as well as you can, and better, if you know how. We had an awning in the middle of the boat on what is called the upper deck, so I managed to swing my grass hammock under that. I then got out my pipe, and sitting down in the cool of the evening, under that tropical sky, nearly five thousand miles away from the dear ones in England, I thought of home.

> "Home! home! sweet, sweet home,
> Wherever I wander, there's no place like home."

I thought of friends at Egerton, at Belmont, at Bolton, at Manchester, at Ashton, in London, &c. As a panorama they passed before me; I saw the busy streets of the great cities and heard again the roar and rattle of the daily traffic, and the silence of these forests almost appalled me. And yet that silence is every now and again broken in upon by some strange cry. There is the "Hoogh! hoogh! hoogh!" like the barking of a dog. It is one of the night owls. Then there is a very plaintive cry as of some one in pain—it is the cry of the weeping monkey; the big bull frog, with his deep, bass croak, now sets up his music, then all is still again. Another moment you hear a big splash in the water; you wonder if some one has fallen in. No! just keep quiet; it is a big fish leaping after its prey. Sometimes you hear a low growl that makes you set your teeth together; and one night, away in the distance, but travelling nearer and nearer, I heard the horrid, bloodthirsty scream of a horde of wild hogs. You know the noise that a pig makes when being pursued? Well, suppose there were a hundred of them, all making that noise together in the dead of the night, with a rising and falling inflection—that will give you some idea of the noise they make. It is simply horrid. It gives you a creepy feeling. The devil is still in the swine. If you are in the forest and meet them, woe be unto you if you can't get up a tree. An Indian told me " A number of us were out hunting one day, and we met a drove of about fifty bush-hogs; up the trees we got at once, and 'bang' went one of our rifles. Bush-hog number one fell over, and the others at once turned upon it, drank its blood and ate it up. When they were satisfied they were going away, but not until they had left us five or six of their carcases for our meal and our trouble."

Having finished my meditations I got into my hammock, and threw a light rug—one of those I got at John Noble's, in Manchester, some seven years ago—over my legs. The heavens were beautiful—a canopy of black set with diamonds. Orion, with his arrows and belt, was bright and clear; right overhead was Jupiter; his brilliance dazzled you—we could just discern his four moons with the naked eye; then Sirius, with his own beauteous light, was a little to the south; and south-east of him, in all its beauty, brightness, and suggestiveness, shone forth the constellation of the Southern Cross. I thought, "Yes, we have the cross ever above us. It is a cross that is alight with heaven's glory. It is not one truth, not one star, but a constellation of truths. It shines for me and for every man. It shines in the darkest night. One star in it points to the north, one to the south, one to the east, one to the west. It has a light for all races and all climes. Its radiance and glory are universal. Keep that cross ever before you." With these thoughts I dozed off, and

> "Sleep, that knits up the ravell'd sleave of care,"

closed my eyes. I must have dozed for some time, when I awoke, feeling damp and chilled. I listened, and there, sure enough, was the patter of rain. My rug was a little wet, and so were my feet. I got up, rubbed myself, and took to a chair. There the sandflies found me. These little creatures sting like very vicious midges on a summer's day at home, only they come upon you in swarms. You feel as you can imagine Gulliver felt when a thousand Brobdignagian arrows pierced his naked body all at once. I would almost sooner have the mosquitoes. Both are bad, and it would puzzle a lawyer to tell which is the worst. We have a proverb here which says,

"Patience, man ride jackass." Well, "patience man had to bear" not "the slings and arrows of outrageous fortune," but the stings and arrows of voracious sandflies until the daylight dawned. About one hour's rest was all I got that night.

Soon after five we are again on our way. There is a freshness in the morning air that sharpens appetite, and as soon as we can we get what is called our "tea," though it is far oftener coffee. "Do you see those tall cabbage-palms?" said the captain. "Yes." "That is where the old fort used to be." Tall and stately those palm trees rise, their heads towering above the topmost branches of the other trees. They are all that remains of a once noted dwelling-place and seat of civilisation. Fort Nassau was for many years the old Dutch capital. There the Governor resided, and on it being reported to him that the enemy's ships were advancing up the river, he, with his people, fled. It is supposed by some that their treasure, being put into an iron chest, was buried somewhere near. An old captain told me he once anchored just opposite Fort Nassau—it is very rare you can do that, for the black sailors say the place is haunted with "jumbies"—and letting his anchor go it fell upon something hard, and wouldn't grip; he hauled it up a bit and shifted it a couple of yards or so to leeward, and down it went into the sand. He didn't know the rumour then of a chest of gold, but he believes now there is a sunken ship there, and it may be Dutch treasure for any one who can fetch it up.

We wanted to land at this place, just to see the ruins of the old brick houses, the rusty cannon, and the graveyard of those old, brave colonists. But they told us the roads were all blocked up, and the place was infested with snakes of the worst kind. "Too much snake," they said, "in the cemetery." The fact is they were afraid of the jumbies, and so did not want to go.

In about three hours we landed at Zeelandia, and as we are about to stay here a few days we will reserve our description for the next chapter.

XIII

AT ZEELANDIA

ZEELANDIA was one of the old Dutch plantations when Fort Nassau was the seat of government. Doubtless, in those days, its cocoa plantations and its coffee plantations were a source of delight to their owners. But it has long since been abandoned. The men and the women, with their toils and their cares, have passed away, but the trees and the forest remain. Of the five hundred acres comprising the estate only a very small portion is now occupied. Over the rest the wild beasts roam at will, and the Indian makes it his hunting ground. Zeelandia to-day is only a small settlement on the Berbice river. It is far away from the town, and the last flickering ray of civilisation hardly finds its way up there and makes its presence felt. A little clearing has been made, and on the bank of the river a solitary house stands. It was dark when we landed. Our little canoe was gliding softly over the water. "Where is the landing-place?" I said. Suddenly a light flashed out from the banks above us. But who is holding it? Not a person could be seen. There the lamp was standing as on a pedestal, shedding its welcome light through the branches of the trees. By and by we saw the outline of a native girl, her hands down by her side, her head erect, and upon the top of her head stood the lamp. "What a splendid lamp-stand she makes," I said. " It is thus that we men should hold up the Lamp of Life. On our heads, supported by our whole manhood, let that Light shine, which lighteth every man that cometh into the world."

Having landed, we look wistfully upon those waters. They are black and deep. As the proverb says, "Saf'ly ribar run deep." By day and by night, solemnly and silently it flows on to the sea. It has made its own channel, it forms its own bank. The River of Life! It flows on, nothing can stop it. Its source is in heaven, it rolls on to the Ocean of Eternity. Every life must make its own channel, find out its own path to the great sea beyond. But we must now enter the little cottage in the wilderness. Though humble and perhaps poor, it is still home. The

Gladstone family can boast of an honoured name, and on the father's side of English descent. J. E. Gladstone was well brought up, and his father gave him a fair education. He served his apprenticeship as an engineer, but he left that calling, preferring the wild, free life of the bush and the forest. He has a numerous family of sons and daughters. They have been brought up respectably and in the fear of God. Through his instrumentality a little chapel was erected at Olandia, on the opposite side of the river. As he had long been a member of the London Missionary Church and for many years a useful deacon, he felt the need of the services of God's house, both for himself, his family, and neighbours. During one of my visits to my Indian stations I was asked to stop and conduct the opening services. This I did. And it was a beautiful sight to see the people who live at different points on the banks of the river come paddling along in their little canoes. Some would come from their lonely little homesteads, miles away, in order to worship God. Our little sanctuary was filled to overflowing. They came as doves to the windows. Their souls thirsted for the water of life. I preached from the text, Acts xvi. 13, "And on the Sabbath we went out of the city, by a river side, where prayer was wont to be made." Afterwards a little Church was formed with about twelve members, and we all partook of the Sacrament. Thus was established this little Bethel in the wilderness; and since that day the good work has gone on.

I remember one very cold winter's night in England. The snow lay thick upon the ground. I had been speaking at a great political meeting. It was late when it was over. I had three miles to walk over the hills. Going into a restaurant I asked for a cup of their best chocolate. It was warm and warming. I thought I never tasted anything better. My dear reader, I am going to take you into a cocoa or chocolate plantation. Follow me along this forest path. Do you see those trees with large, dark-green, undivided leaves? Those are the cocoa trees. They are not very tall, only about eighteen or twenty feet high. But they have many branches, the branches growing out from the stem about six feet from the ground, and these often covered with large, clustered flowers. The fruit is like a cucumber in shape, or like a vegetable marrow, and is about eight inches long. Some of them are yellow and others a reddish-brown, according to the kind of tree. They weigh from one to two pounds. As they hang from the boughs they look lovely. The ancients might well call this genus of plants " Theobroma," which means " Food of the gods." When the fruit is ripe it is taken down, and on opening it a large number of seeds of a pale reddish-brown colour are found. These seeds, not unlike our large beans in shape, are put in the sun to dry. They are then pounded, and, mixed with a little sugar, a delicious chocolate is made. It is not an uncommon thing to see a diligent black woman in one of our villages seated upon the ground and vigorously pounding away at some of these cocoa beans. In a very short time they will produce for you a delicious and nourishing stick of chocolate. Cocoa trees grow here without any trouble. We even find them growing wild on the banks of the river. Many a large pod have I plucked whilst paddling up the river with the Indians in the canoe.

Not far from the cocoa trees is the coffee plantation. A walk through it when the trees are in bloom is charming, for the scent from the flowers is simply delicious. The trees are not very large, only about twelve feet high, with branches shooting out almost from the ground. The leaves are evergreen, shiny, oblong, and leathery. The flowers are in clusters, like a bunch of apple-blossom, and white as snow. They send forth a beautiful fragrance. The fruit or berries are of a

AT ZEELANDIA

dark red colour. A plantation will have sometimes as many as five hundred trees. As the coffee tree loves the shade and plenty of moisture, it is not uncommon to have growing around them the sandbox tree, or fruit trees that have long spreading branches, to screen them from the heat of the sun. The coffee tree continues flowering for eight months in the year, and so two or three crops are gathered annually. Coffee was exported from Berbice in large quantities some years ago. In 1803 nearly ten millions of pounds (9,954,610 lbs.) was sent out of the colony. Twenty years after it had fallen down to eight millions, and twenty years after that to 2,139,430 lbs. Now it is but a few thousands. But the people are beginning to realise that the time has come when this industry ought to be revived. The old coffee plantations are becoming objects of interest and desire. Nowhere does the coffee tree flourish so well as here. The Rev. T. Veness, in his " El Dorado," tells of a coffee field up the Essequebo, planted at a period unknown, which still continues to bear in abundance, "Nature alone in this fertile soil keeping up a reproduction of the trees."

Further aback are the rice fields. These are on low-lying ground and in swampy places. For the rice likes plenty of water. Indeed, it is after the heavy rains, when the land is submerged, that the sowing begins. As in the olden days "they cast their bread (*i.e.*, their rice) upon the waters, and they find it after many days." Rice is known here to yield as much as three hundred-fold. A friend of mine up in this same district counted as many as 450 on one stalk. Nothing looks more lovely than a field of rice when it has just begun to grow. The tender blade is of such a bright, fresh, rich green. When the reaping time comes, it is one of great joy. They that have gone forth weeping, bearing their precious seed, come again rejoicing, bringing their sheaves with them. After the grain has been gathered, it has to be threshed and winnowed. They have no machines to do this, so it has to be done by hand. The process is a very tedious one, and the labour heavy. As we have rice every morning to breakfast, it being used as a "side dish," and again to dinner, the black servants have to do this. I went into the threshing room and watched them at work. They had a large wooden mortar, made out of a tree trunk and standing about two feet high, and two wooden pestles, three feet long, and weighing about eight pounds.

The grain is put into the mortar. Then the pounding begins. 'One on each side, bringing down their pestle with great force, stroke for stroke, just as you have seen two smiths striking on the anvil. The husk being thus broken, they put it into a basket-work sieve and blow the chaff away. I thought how forcibly they illustrate the words, "The ungodly are like the chaff which the wind driveth away."

Having now looked around, and feeling somewhat weary, it is time for us to return. As we are hanging our hammocks at the son's house, a little further down the river, we must either walk along a narrow path through the forest, or take the canoe. As the latter will be easier we will go that way. The little house which you see is right in the midst of the forest. A space has been cleared for it a few yards round, but there are no roads to it or from it. The deep, silent river rolls at its base The "Hermitage," like all houses in the river district, is a kind of combination of house and benaab. It has no doors, or windows, or chimneys, but consists of upright posts, with a paling round. These palings are about four feet high, and are made of "wattles" out of the manicole-palm. They allow the little breeze which we get to have full play, and thus help to keep the place cool. There is a boarded floor about three feet from the ground. The roof is made of Dehalibani leaves, a species of the palm tree. The lady of the house, knowing that the minister would want a resting-place, like the good woman of Shunem, fitted up and set apart one room as "the prophet's room." The old prophet had only "a bed, a table, a stool, and a candlestick" (see 2 Kings iv. 10). Modern prophets require a little more.

Poor Oliver Goldsmith! He died in April—this very month—about a hundred and twenty-two years ago. Walpole called him "an inspired idiot," and Garrick describes him as one

"... for shortness call'd Noll,
Who wrote like an angel, and talk'd like poor Poll."

Have you read that charming poem of his called "The Hermit"? There are two lines in it I want to quote; they are the last two of this verse—

" Then pilgrims turn, thy cares forego;
All earthborn cares are wrong;
*Man wants but little here below,
Nor wants that little long.*"

Come and live in the wilderness here and you will find how true it is. Man's desires are many, his *real necessities* are few. John the Baptist got on very well with his leathern girdle, and his locusts and wild honey. Up here a man only needs a shirt and a pair of trousers. A Benaab covered with leaves is cosy enough for his hammock. A fish caught in the stream, a bird shot in the bush, fruit from the wild trees, appeases appetite and satisfies hunger. For his books, he has Nature's volumes, he—

> "Finds tongues in trees, books in the running brooks,
> Sermons in stones, and good in everything."

It is the civilisation of the city, with its social obligations and its artificial conditions of existence, that enslaves men and makes them the dupes of inordinate desires. In Nature's simplicity is *grandeur, reality, freedom,* and *power.*

Our little room, though only a few feet wide, is large enough to rest in.

> "Tired nature's sweet restorer, balmy sleep,"

comes on her downy pinions, and closes our eyes more readily there than in many a city mansion. The moon with her mild sweet face is our candle, and the whistling chorus of the insects is the music that lulls us to sleep. That first night in the forest I shall never forget. At dusk the six-o'clock beetle began with his shrill whistle. By half-past six it was quite dark. A whole chorus of sounds now fills the air. There's the whistle of a steam engine, the train is approaching the station—No! that cannot be, it is the *sun beetle,* telling us of his approach. Then there's the scissors grinder—a beetle that makes a noise just like the scissors grinder in the streets at home—and the sawyer beetle, busy at work on some branch of a tree and making a noise like that which a circular steam saw makes, and the great borer, worming his way into the trunk of a tree; sitting on one of the branches of a tree is the "candle beetle," giving forth his light so that the others can see to do their work. There are black beetles and brown beetles and blue beetles and green beetles and rhinoceros and staghorn beetles—they are of all sizes up to a duck-egg. Then there are grasshoppers and locusts and cockroaches and walking leaves and praying prophets, all singing and shouting and working; then there are the tree frogs and the water frogs, all whistling and croaking like mad, the big bull frog not unlike the bellowing of an ox, the tree frogs shouting "Burra-bararoo," the others, "Kroak! kroak!" Then there's the bark of the owl, and the scream of the parrot (screecher) and the "Ha! ha! ha!" of the goshawk, and the plaintive whistle of the weeping monkey. The whole atmosphere is alive with sound—you are in the midst of a vast humming host of buzzing, burring, screeching, hissing, whistling, croaking insects. Yet you cannot see one of them. All that you can see is a dim outline of big trees, dark and sombre with here and there flashes of light from the flitting fireflies. They are on the leaves of the trees, emitting sparks from their bodies that flash like diamonds; they are on the ground at our feet like crystallised dew drops; they are darting through the air like shooting stars. In the midst of it all I stood. By and by the moon rose up behind the forest. She cast her silvery rays on bush and bower, weird shadows lurked among the trees; that dark object on the ground might be a coiled cobra ready to spring; that rustle in the thicket might be a crouching tiger. Springing out of the grass there is an iguana; a yawarri is hidden up that tree; a lizard has just run past your feet and darted down this hole; you feel as if you dare not stir; above and below are things of life, and it may be things of death. For no poison is so deadly as that of the little green parrot snake or the labarri that crawls at your feet. My daughter, who was with me, occupied the little room. This evening I slung my hammock upstairs. In her diary she says, " In the night, by the light of the moon, I could see the huge cockroaches crawling up the walls, and two or three spiders, with legs two inches long, creeping on the roof close above my head. I opened the little shutter which served as a window and looked out. Before me was the great forest, dark and sombre, with the moonbeams shining through the trees and casting weird shadows all around. I could hear the buzzing and whistling of the insects, the loud croak of the great bull frog, with his whistling companions all around him. The hoot of the night owl, the scream of the monkeys after the fruit, and the distant bark or howl of the crab dog. These are the sights and sounds that fell upon my ear as I stood by that opening, a hundred and forty miles from the nearest town, and around the great primeval forest, with the great dark river flowing just below. That is the time when one thinks of home and loved ones and friends, and thank God that there is a loving heavenly Father whose watchful eye never sleeps, and who is guarding them and us.

The next day was a wet day. And it may be said with truth here, " It never rains but it pours." We sat in what might be called the little open verandah and watched the heavy rain-drops, as they pattered upon the leaves of the trees. Hanging over the wattles was a huge tiger skin. We had arrived a few days after the fellow was killed. Tell us about it, I said, for like the Athenians of old we had nothing else to do just then but to tell or to hear some new thing. "Well," said Alec, " nebba trouble

INUNDATED FOREST.

trouble till trouble trouble you. Dis fellow trouble a' we too much. He came in de night and steal de pork. He came 'gain and take a' we fowl. So we say, ' We no clea' groun' fo' monkey fo' run 'pon, and we no rear fowl fo' tigah to eat. So we must ketch he one dem nights.' Three of us get we guns, we climb 'pon tree, and we wait and we say, ' Ebery day debil help tief, one day God mus' help watchman.' By and by we hear noise, massa, tigah come carrying big hog 'tween he teet'. Bang! Tigah stops, tigah growl. Bang! Tigah roll ober. He keep still, but we say, ' Ebery shut eye no a sleep.' We gib he one more. Bang! He dead fo' true. We haul he up. Dere he skin. ' No ketchee, no habee.' "

We measured the skin and it was seven feet seven inches from snout to tail. We got two of the teeth, which we have here; each one was nearly three inches long. These formidable molars—I call 'em mawlers—in such a powerful jaw would soon let daylight into a man, and crackle his bones. We were very glad to have his skin.

In the afternoon, as the rain had cleared off, we took to the canoes and crossed the river to the little chapel. From thence with our "nets" and cutlasses and bowie knives and guns and dogs we went into the forest.

The forest on that side is very thick with trees, and noted for its wild beasts. But they come out mostly at night. A good dog is a good protection. Not that he is a match for either "boas, or tigers, or jaguars, or bushmasters," but by his scent and quickness of hearing he can detect their lurking places, and he never fails to give you timely warning. But many of these little creatures become the prey of these forest roaming monsters.

Horatio Gladstone, with whom we were staying, had a dog—a fine bull-terrier, full of pluck and go. If he had been blessed with a little discretion it would have been better for him. But he would tackle anything. One day, running in the bush near the water, he roused a large water boa. For a moment he stood, and, facing it, barked, the next it came down upon him with its mouth wide open, and just swallowed him alive. "We thought we heard him barking inside," said Alec, but we hadn't our guns with us, and so we had to make off. We have never seen him since.

It was in this forest that one of the men was bitten by the "bushmaster." This is one of the most dreaded of our snakes. It is about eight feet long, and has a terrible mouth and fangs. Its poison is said to be very deadly. In fact, it is dreaded both by man and beast. If you meet it you must either kill it or be killed. Flight is impossible, for it can run faster than you, and it can climb up a tree. There is only one thing you can do, and that is cross the water if you be near either river or creek, and even there it will follow you sometimes. Of course, the best thing is to shoot it. But sometimes a man has no gun. On this occasion the man was looking in a hole for a labba, when out sprang this snake. As quick as possible he turned and struck it with his cutlass, but before he could step aside, the head of the snake already severed from the body, bit him in the heel. He sung out to his mates, and made for the boat on the river side—in five minutes he staggered like a drunken man. "My eyes," he said, "grew dark; they got hold of me and put me in the boat." Now, luckily, there lived close by a man called Barker, who is known as a snake charmer. He seems to have a wonderful power over all the snake tribe. There is not one, I am assured, that he will not take up in his hands. He knows the antidote to all their poisons. "This man," he said, "gave me some medicine. I thought I was dead. My head nearly burst with pain; my eyes were dark, but by and by perspiration came on, and there oozed out through my skin a white substance like sawdust or very small shavings. I began to recover.

But it was months ere I was myself again. The mark of the wound is still on my foot, and I pray God I may never pass through the like again. Since that day the sight of a snake almost makes me tremble."

As we were walking through the forest, one behind another, we saw a great silk cotton tree. This is one of the largest trees of the forest. It grows to a height of one hundred feet, and is twelve or fourteen feet in diameter. The branches do not begin to grow from the trunk till it has attained a height of about sixty feet. It only blossoms once in three years. The bud contains a fine silk cotton of a light grey colour, hence its name. The humming birds use this "silk cotton" to line their nests with. In connection with this tree there are many superstitions. The people believe it to be the abode of departed spirits. The guardian spirit of the Cumaka, or silk cotton tree, walks around it at mid-day and at twelve o'clock at night. The Rev. John Wray, who laboured here in 1818, says, "On the site for the new chapel, and exactly opposite the house, was a large silk cotton tree which stood in the way." For some time Mr. Wray could get no one with courage enough to cut it down, for the negroes held the tree in great veneration, and feared to offend its spirit. So at last the parson said, " That tree has got to come down, and if you won't cut it down, I will," and, taking off his coat, he seized the axe and commenced the work. The men looked on for some minutes, and seeing that Mr. Wray was not afraid, and that *he* was the real transgressor, they took courage, and coming for the axe they began to cut, but at every stroke they cried out, " No me da massa, no me da massa." Thus the tree was brought to the ground. Some say that the juice of the tree is red like blood, others that there is a gaseous exhalation from the tree when cut, which is very injurious, and that these have given rise to the superstition.

However, we noticed as we passed this Cumaka tree in the forest, a kind of bush rope ladder, leading up to its branches. " What is that for ? " I said. " That is the tree we often climb up, sitting and waiting for game. I have sat hours upon hours in that tree, and have brought home many a bird for the pot, and many a bush-hog for the feast."

But now we must return. We have been where cultivation, even in the old days, never found its way.

"This is the forest primeval. The murmuring pines and the hemlocks
Bearded with moss, and in garments green, indistinct in the twilight."

XIV

KIMBIA LAKES

'AN' you, missie, been to dat Kimbia Lake? We creoles no able fo' go dere. Dat place too much bad. Too much snake in de grass, and too much tigah, and too much bad ebery ting. We so glad you come back safe." Such was the greeting we got from our black creole friends on our return. Indeed it was only when we got back to town that we found out what a dangerous place we had been in. One person who has lived in the upper reaches of the river for years, and is well acquainted with bush and forest, said that Kimbia Lake was a very dangerous place for any one to go to. In fact very few people ever went there. Its wild beasts were noted for their fierceness. There being little food to be got at certain seasons of the year, hunger made them ravenous, and then they would attack anything. The place abounds with large serpents; some of these twenty feet long have been seen floating upon the water. " I wouldn't have dared to go up there," said a friend. " You English ladies have plenty of courage." This was to my daughter who is, I believe, the first English lady that has visited it. The fact is we were quite unconscious of any special danger we were running into; dangers peculiar to the creek and forest and bush and savannah we were prepared for.

Our trust was in God, and He was our shield. As the wise man says, " He is a shield unto them that put their trust in Him " (Prov. xxx. 5). Besides this I had a kind of feeling that one's life is not his own; it is in God's keeping. We cannot shun a danger that is appointed, nor can we incur one that is not.

> " On two days it steads not to run from thy grave,
> The appointed and the unappointed day;
> On the first neither balm nor physician can save,
> Nor thee on the second the universe slay."

The morning of our starting out was lovely. Getting up with the first streaks of dawn we had our bath and our "cawfee," making the latter as substantial as we could with eggs and rice and cassava. Bidding them goodbye at Zeelandia, we walked down to the river and got into the boat.

There were four good strong native pullers. We had a captain at the bow, and a steersman behind, besides myself, my daughter, a black servant called Zoo, and the Rev. J. S. We had equipped ourselves with all needful things. "Be sure," I said, "to put the guns in." So we had our guns, our bows and arrows, such as the Indians use, our cutlasses, our axes, and our bowie knives. Our lunch basket also was well packed. At the word "ready" we pushed out from the landing, and our journey commenced.

How still everything seemed that morning as we paddled softly down the side of the great river! Not a breath of air is stirring. The leaves on the trees are as motionless as if they were carved in stone. A little canoe with one solitary occupant is coming towards us. It is a lonely squatter journeying to his rice-fields a little further up the river, or he is going to look at his fishing-line and his traps which he set last night. "Morning, Buddie! how you do?" "So, so! how *you* do." Such is the greeting that opens up a little "talkee" on points of interest to these dwellers in the wilderness. They have no postman coming with his letters of joy and of sorrow, no daily papers with its gossip of the world, no cablegrams telling them that the Tsar slept soundly last night, and the

Kaiser was learning to walk the tight-rope, and the President of the American Republic in a fit of patriotism had insulted John Bull and challenged the man in the moon. Their nerves are never unstrung with news about the awful condition of the people in Timbuctoo, and their appetite is not affected by the advance of the Matabeles and the uncompromising attitude of the Boers.

In answer to our question, the captain tells us that we have only one more "point" and then we shall come to the creek. They measure distance on the river by "points," that is, by the different bends of the stream. There are long points, and short points, and half points, no two points measuring exactly the same. Ask how far it is to such a place, and they will say, "Two long points and a short one," or "Three points and a half." It is only when you have become accustomed to the bends of the river that you can measure the distance to a place by its points. And now we come to a little opening in the trees. It only looks a few feet wide. The overhanging branches with their thick foliage and their intertwined lianos almost hiding it from view. As we enter, that little opening expands, the trees on either side are statelier and taller, their great spreading branches stretch out towards each other as if to shake hands, forming a leafy canopy over our heads, the water is blacker, the shade is deeper, on each side the forest stands, we are in Kimbia Creek.

Being fond of a little paddling myself, and wishing to relieve one of the men, I took off my coat and rolled up my sleeves and began. The simultaneous stroke of the paddles in the water, sometimes so soft that you cannot hear them, and at other times loud like the tramping of feet, makes a kind of music. You feel inclined to sing, to whistle, to beat time. You must fall into the rhythm and the motion.

> We sail along through Kimbia Creek,
>   All friends, both good and true ;
> The monkeys whistle, the parrots squeak,
>   As we paddle our own canoe.
>
> We care not now for the big, big world,
>   What *it* may say or do ;
> We wonder and muse, we've a quiet untold,
>   As we paddle our own canoe.
>
> The toucan cries, and "pai-pai-o,"
>   Vibrates the forest through;
> We watch the love-birds come and go,
>   As we paddle our own canoe.
>
> So here's to the wild, free, forest life,
>   With its skies so bright and blue ;
> Far away from the world's unrest and strife,
>   We paddle our own canoe.

KIMBIA LAKES

The dog Leo which we took with us has been sent ashore, he is running in the forest alongside of the creek ; now he is off on a scent; he does not, however, go far into the forest, he is afraid of Massa Tigah. "He too coward," says one of the men. I suggested that he was hungry, for he certainly was very thin. "Daag magah, he head big"—*i.e.* Dog thin, or as they say "maugre," has a big head. Then I said "Feed him!" "No, massa, Daag wha' a bring a bone, sa carry ain," so he must run in the bush and hunt. Sometimes he scents something afar off, and at the same time something starts up at the creek side ; he follows the other and misses this ; if he had only followed this we should have got it, and the other he has no chance at, it is off beyond his speed. We feel inclined to be "bex." *Cui bono?* To what good? "Daag hab four foot, but can't walk on four roads wan time." There's a labba ! Up with your gun ! He's off ! With a big splash he plunges into the water. "Down with the boat, boys," softly, "he may come up again." We sit as silent as grim death, the boat floats with the stream, guns are loaded, capped and ready, but master labba keeps well out of the way. We have not time to wait, so we give up the chase with the solemn reflection : "Ebery day fishing day, but ebery day no ketchin' day."

Once more we are paddling up-stream, but the creek is getting narrower, here and there are fallen trees, right athwart our path. Some are well under water so that we can just skim over the tops of them, others are above water, forming a bridge for the monkeys to cross over. There's a monkey, do you see him. Ah, the fellow! See how he runs up that tree. He's looking at us and chuckling. " Mo' monkey climb, mo' he show he tail." Point the gun at him. He's off to the topmost branch. He can curl himself up into a small compass like a ball, and there he hides behind a big leaf. Monkey can't be found. "Ah! monkey knows wha' tree he a climb 'pon." "Those monkeys," says Alec, the black boy, "are too cunning; see how they stick to a nut or a 'cherry' when they get one, afraid if you make the least move that they are going to lose it. He eats it looking round as if he were not sure of it till he'd swallowed it. Hence our proverb, 'Monkey say, "Wha' deh a-me belly a-me own ; wha' deh a-me mout" a yackman want.'" " Have you ever seen a monkey laugh?" "No." " Well, I have one at home; we call him Sambo, but the black people call him Jack, and I have seen him laugh many a time. You tickle him or please him with anything, and he will put his two hands on his sides and bend down and shake just like a

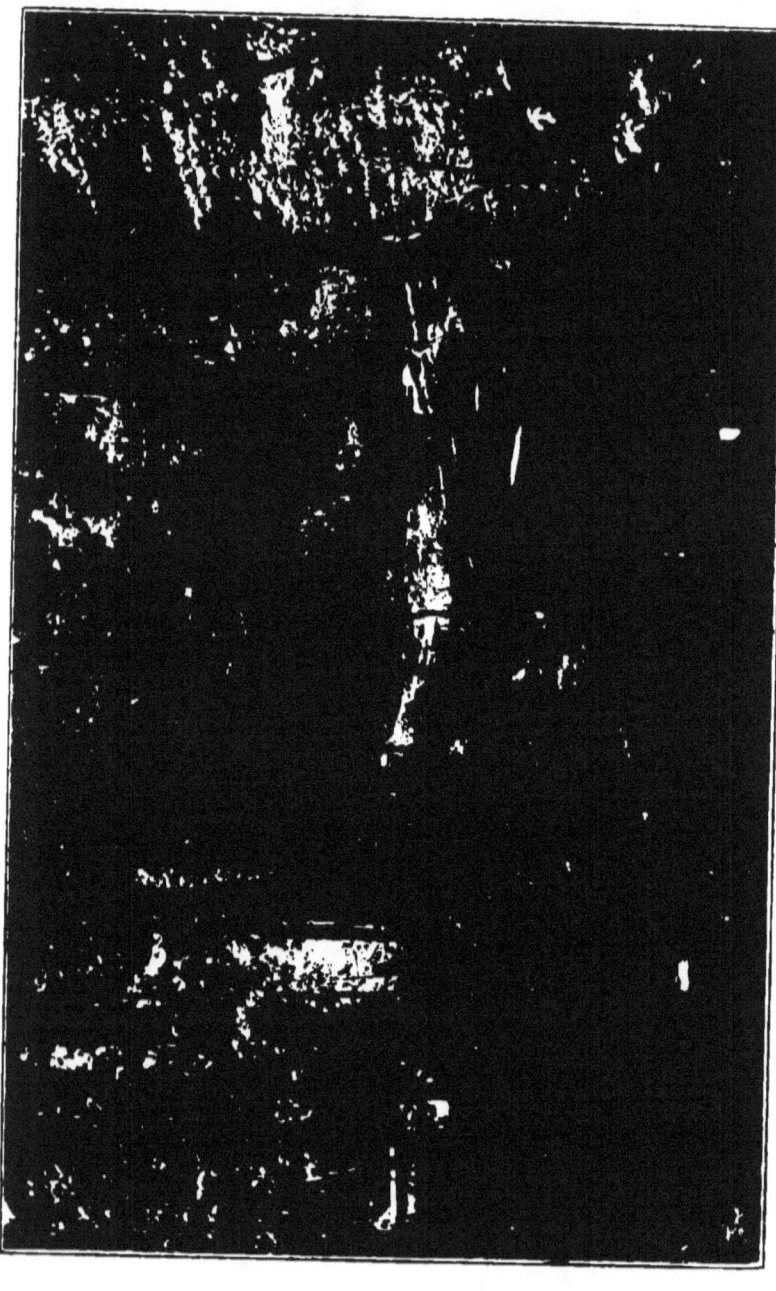

CREEK, WITH TIGER'S BRIDGE.

person in a fit of laughter, and at the same time a broad grin will steal over his face showing all his front teeth. I tell you he looks too funny." "But have you ever seen him cry?" said Alec. "Well, I've heard him wail and lament, but I never saw him take his handkerchief out of his pocket and wipe his tears away."

> "If you want see monkey cry,
> Tick a peppa in he eye."

But here's a Dutchman's bridge, *i.e.*, a tree trunk across the creek; we shall have to get under. At the word "duck" we all lie down flat in the bottom of the boat, and we manage to get through safe. But this is dangerous work, for it is often on such trees that venomous snakes are to be found. These fallen trees are becoming more numerous as we advance, and great branches sticking up impede our progress. Our cutlasses are now in constant requisition. Whilst giving a final stroke to one stiff hard branch, my cutlass fell out of my hand into the water. Luckily it stuck in the mud, point downwards, like an arrow in a target; so getting a long stick with a slit in the end we managed to pull the cutlass up. But now we are stopped again, here is a tree trunk that our boat is unable to pass under. There's nothing for it but to cut the thing away, so we bring the boat up close and fetch out the big axe; in a few minutes the way is again clear and we are off. We have now been paddling about six hours and feel ready for a rest; so we pull up and get out in the forest, and have a few sandwiches and some creek water. Then we light our pipes, and smoke that very weed which God makes to grow in these very forests, and we talk and think of many things. We do not go far from one another, for it is not safe, and the dog keeps watch for us by running round.

In about another hour we reach the edge of the forest on our left hand, the trees get thinner, and the light begins to break in. We stop, and walking a short way through the bush, a splendid view stretches out before us. Imagine the two sides of a square, or rather oblong, and your standing at the angle where the two sides meet, up one side is the line of the great forest, stretching away miles upon miles and running parallel with the great river; up the other side is a thin line of foliage skirting the bank of the creek, and right in front, far as the eye can see, is the vast savannah. It rises towards the centre into an eminence forming a ridge of high ground. You reach this, and again stretching out before you is a grand, wild prospect of tableland. Over this the wild deer bound, and towards the Corentyne coast the wild cattle roam. The tiger lurks in the long grass for his prey, and the reptiles make it their hiding-place. But now we are coming to the head of the lake. The stream is narrower and beautifully clear. The moco moco grow so thick as seriously to threaten our progress, but determination overcomes difficulties. We drive our boat through them, dodging in and out like a dog at a fair; at last, about 2.15, Kimbia Lake bursts upon our view. It is a fine sheet of water about three miles long and two broad, or even more in the rainy season—its waters dark and solemn, but sweet and clear. Around it rises the high ground of the savannah, with bunches of palm trees here and there; these Ita palms, with their tall stems and their waving plumes, making a picture of beauty in themselves. To our right as we entered the forest ran out to a point, and formed a little hill covered with trees. The banks of the lake were covered with tall grass, reeds, and rushes. These rose to a height of five or six feet. In the rainy season these are doubtless all under water. On entering the lake one of the men shot an Indian arrow up into the air, so as to alight further on in the water, and it may be shoot a fish, but we found the arrow a little later floating on the surface. The one thing that impressed us most was the weird silence of the place; a silence as of death reigned around; it became oppressive. We sat in the boat and seemed at moments unable to speak; not a breath of wind stirred, not a leaf moved. We were on an enchanted lake. The sun shone hot and fierce above our heads, the waters were like a sheet of smoked glass. The place was surely haunted. At any moment one could imagine the witches of Macbeth rising solemnly out of the dense morass and crying :—

> "Black spirits and white,
> Red spirits and grey,
> Mingle, mingle, mingle,
> You that mingle may."

We sailed round the lake, we went up one of the streams that flow into it from somewhere in the vicinity of Canje Creek, and then, after getting a few specimens of the wild grasses, we turned our boat's head towards home. "Plenty of sport here," said one of the men, "in the hunting season. Fish too many in this lake. Stop till night, and we'll have too much to take home." But this we could not do, and as we were all getting fagged with the excessive heat, and wanted our insides replenishing, we made our way as quick as we could to a nice camping ground in the forest. There we lit a fire and put our kettle on to boil. In a short time we had some tea ready, Miss Lilian and the black servant superintending the feast.

On our return down the stream we found considerable difficulty arising from the fact that with the ebbing tide the water had fallen three feet. This brought many of the logs that were well under as we went up so near the surface that our boat would sometimes stick on them, and the men had to get out on the log and push it over. On two or three occasions the boat heeled over, and it was only by a kind of miracle that we were not completely capsized. After some three hours' hard work, I called a halt, and handed my drinking cup round to the men, when one of them accidentally let it fall into the water. At first we could see the cup, which was of a bright metal, and we tried with a stick to get it. But we found the water was so deep, and the stick had to be so long that we could not manage it. At last Alec, who had let it fall, said, " I will go in for it." So with his flannel and pants on he dived in, but he said the current was so strong and the mud so slippery that he was carried away from where the cup lay. There was a depth of between ten and twelve feet of water, and we were not more than eight feet from the side. Swimming ashore, he cut a long pole, and hauling the boat over the spot we stuck it in the ground and held it there, then Alec went down holding on to the pole. At last he got hold of the cup; we watched but he did not seem to offer to come up again; he seemed half dazed. Shaking the pole we cried, "Come up, man!"—and to our relief we soon saw him rising, and we pulled him into the boat.

We now found it getting dark. This, with the half-submerged logs and the broken branches projecting up out of the water made our travelling both difficult and dangerous. It now needed every one to take the paddle that could, and be prepared for any emergency. "If you are upset," I said, "and pitched into the water, make for the bank, and if you cannot swim, get hold of some branch of a tree."

On and on we go. The six o'clock beetle begins, the last rays of the setting sun shine through the increasing gloom of the forest. The trees begin to look like dark objects with their arms spread out; the water becomes inky black. All is dark as night around; a little light can be seen as we look up through the opening over our heads. It is the light of the stars.

> "There is no light in earth or heaven
> But the cold light of stars,
> And the first watch of the night is given
> To the red planet Mars."

KIMBIA LAKES

By and by the moon rises, weird shadows seem to walk amid the trees, and flit across the waters. Round and round we go, is there no end to this winding creek? Our arms are wearied with the paddles, our eyes ache with straining them to see in the dark, our backs feel as if they would break with sitting so long in one position. Suddenly the light increases, an opening appears, the full moon shines on the broad waters of the Berbice river. Now we are all right. Soon we shall be home. That night we needed no music to lull us off to sleep. Getting into our hammocks we soon passed into that state of unconsciousness—

> "Where the wicked cease from troubling,
> And the weary are at rest."

ABARYBANNA OR KIMBIA LAKE.

Far, far up the Berbice river,
   Far from city, far from town,
From amid the unknown regions
   There a stream flows gently down.

Rolling down through bush and forest,
   Where no human foot hath trod,
Making for itself a pathway
   Destined for it by its God.

Through this hot and unknown country,
   Which few human eyes have seen,
On it flows, 'mid sunbeams glancing,
   And the foliage rich and green.

BRITISH GUIANA

Sailing 'neath the fluttering leaflets,
  Hanging from the forest trees,
We with hope our boat pushed onward
  Aided by the gentle breeze.

The toucan echoed through the forest
  With his wild and piercing cry,
And the monkeys in the tree-top
  Grinned at us as we went by.

Suddenly a beauteous vision
  Rose before our wondering eyes,
There fair Kimbia's lake lay nestling
  'Neath the pale and azure skies.

All around the prairie hillocks
  Rose as if to guard it well,
And the coarse brown jungle grasses
  With the breezes rose and fell.

There the stately Royal Ita
  Waved its plumes amid the wind,
And the bamboo's slender tendrils
  Modestly stood up behind.

As we gazed around in rapture
  All was silent as the night,
Not a leaflet stirred around us,
  Yet the sun shone hot and bright.

Quiet reigned and ghostly stillness,
  Not a living thing seemed there,
Yet beneath those jungle grasses
  Slept the wild beast in his lair.

In some quiet corner sleeping
  Lies the deadly cobra coiled,
And the twisting, sleek camoudi
  Will not have his purpose foiled.

KIMBIA LAKES

Now's the time when beasts and reptiles
   Take their mid-day rest and ease ;
But when comes the stilly twilight,
   Then they creep beneath the trees.

When at night the moonbeams glisten
   Far o'er the savannah wild,
Comes the shrill cry of the monkey,
   As of some poor, suffering child.

From some dark recess the tiger
   Rushes forth with savage growl,
And as stealthy as a serpent
   There the jaguar does prowl.

All these dangers lurked around us,
   Yet we did not seem to fear,
For we knew that One above us
   Ever watched, was ever near.

We were trusting in that presence
   Which we could not hear or see,
And we knew that He would keep us
   From all harm and danger free.

In the town and in the city,
   Wheresoe'er our way we take,
We shall ne'er forget the vision
   Of fair Kimbia's lovely lake.

                       L. E. C.

XV

AMONG THE ARAWAACK INDIANS

IT was very early in the morning when we got into our canoe and paddled our way to the river-boat which was lying at anchor in mid-stream. Everything was fresh and green. The heavy dew was still lying upon grass and shrub. Indeed, everything was saturated with its moisture. We found a large number, chiefly negroes from the town, on their way up to the wood-cutting grants in the interior. From these we received a cheery "Good-morning, parson," and I went round to them all, giving them a little tract to read, and after a little service and many kindly words, we took our place on the upper deck. We now came to the sand-hills, which takes its name from the hills of sand which skirt the banks of the river. Here there is a neat little Anglican church, which calls the scattered worshippers from the surround-

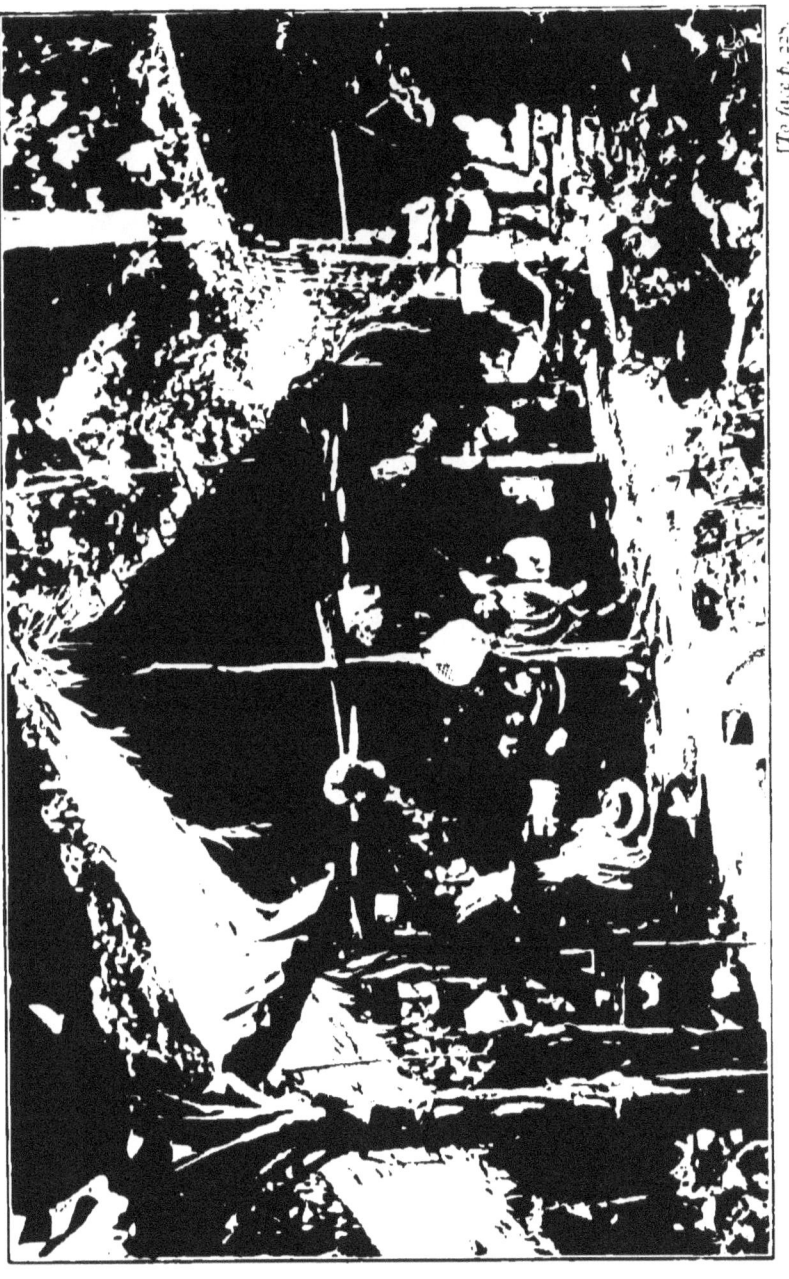

INDIAN BENAUB (ARAWAACKS).

ing district, and ministers to the spiritual needs of these dwellers in the wilderness.

Our next place of note is "Maria Henrietta," where the London Missionary Society have had a mission for many years. And soon after we come to Coomacka. This is as far as the river-boat goes.

Coomacka takes its name from the large silk cotton (coomacka) trees that there abound. The river here is wide and deep. There is a feeling of solitude about the place, and a look of wildness. We have reached the ultimate point of civilisation. From under the trees a number of canoes begin to emerge. These canoes are from six to twelve or fifteen feet in length, and from a foot and a half to two or three feet in width. They are cut out of the trunk of a tree, and "kittle cattle" they are to get into. The least step on one side and over you go. I saw one man overbalance himself, and in a moment the canoe went down, and the only thing to be seen was the man swimming in the water towards the shore. The sight of these canoes was most picturesque. There were about twenty of them, and sitting most composedly in them were a number of Indians, men and women and children, each with his little paddle in his hand. The chief came up first. He shook me by the hand,

and in broken English bade me welcome. The other Indian men followed suit. They then began to collect our baggage and tow it away, some in one canoe and some in another. In the centre of the chief's boat they had made a little tent of Dehalibani leaves to screen the parson from the intense heat of the sun. Having carefully got down into the canoe, not without some misgiving, I seated myself down on a cross board in the middle. Keeping myself very still, the word of command was given, and we began to paddle away, seven or eight canoes in the front, and the rest in the rear. With wonderful strength and agility they used their little Indian paddles; there would be eight or ten or twelve paddles to a canoe, all of them striking the water in concert. As you looked at them from behind, they looked like the simultaneous steps of an army on the march, the paddles being the legs of the boats. When they wanted to go softly, as they do when fishing or hunting, the word was given, and each paddle dipped into the water with a silence and stealth that enabled them to come close up to their prey. For hours they will keep up this paddling without apparent exertion or exhaustion. I have set out with them at four o'clock in the morning, and we have travelled on all day till six in the evening, with only a little break or two for water and refreshment. All that they seem to eat is a little cassava cake, washed down with the water of the river. After about two hours we turned out of the Berbice river into the Wikky Creek. This stream, though called a creek, is wider than the Irwell and much deeper. We are now fairly out of the track of civilisation. The Indians are at home here. We are travelling through their happy hunting-ground. On each side of us stood in primitive grandeur the magnificent trees of the forest, their branches bending over and dipping into the dark waters of this unknown stream. There were the " green heart, the purple heart, the simaruba," the wallabah, the mora, the yarruroo, and many other trees. The prospect grew wilder as we advanced. Winding in and out we found ourselves in the very heart of the forest. The stream begins to get narrower; occasionally a huge tree trunk, forty or fifty feet in length, lying right across the creek, disputes our progress, but skimming round it or shooting under it we still go on our way. After about five hours' good pulling the chief says, " Do you see those tall bamboos? That is the place where we land." With a sudden turn we shot under the branches of the trees, and there in that little opening stood a number of Indian women and picknies. Their attire was of the simplest kind, one garment sufficing in some cases to cover their person.

The Bucks, that is the name given to the male Indian, and Buckeen, or Bokeen, to the female, are divided into many tribes. Some of these are well known, and others hardly known at all. The tribes best known are the Arawaacks, the Accawais, the Caribs, the Warraus, and the Macoosis. In addition to these are the Arecunas, the Wapisianas, the Woyawais, the Attorias, the Powsianas, &c., &c. Some have estimated their number in the colony at 10,000, 15,000, 20,000, and 25,000.

The best known are the five first named. Of these it may be interesting to give some little account. And first of all, of their general history, we may say it is a blank. They themselves can tell us nothing of it. They have no writings and few traditions. The latter are so vague and incoherent that very little can be made of them. No record of achievement or memorial of glory lights up their past. It is a page on which nothing has been written. Whence they came, history knows not; it can only conjecture. How long they have been here we can only surmise. With the discovery of the continent comes the discovery of its strange inhabitants. He was found there a dweller in the forest with the parrot, the monkey, the camoude, and the jaguar. With the trees of the forest he grew, with the trees of the forest he died, and with the trees of the forest he still lives. He is a stranger to the rest of mankind. Roaming through the vast forests of the interior, hunting his deer, his bush hog, and his fish, he is altogether ignorant of the vast world of humanity buzzing around him. Even those who live upon our borders, and have been reached by our missionaries, know not the day of the week or the year of our Lord. As for time, that is measured by sunrise and sunset. For hundreds of years they have lived the same apathetic, indifferent, unaspiring life. The fulfilment of an instinct, the gratification of a passion, sum up the round of their existence. They eat, they sleep, they hunt, they laugh, they cry, they die, and their bodies return to the earth from whence they came· The general appearance of these Indians is pretty much the same. They are of a reddish brown, not unlike new and clean copper. Some, of course, are a little lighter in colour, and some a little darker. They are short in stature, but thickly built and fleshy. The women are somewhat less in size than the men, and some of them are very short. They have long, straight, coarse black hair, the Bokeen wearing it loose hanging over the shoulders, except those in our mission, who have begun to plait it and tie it up. Their features are regular, but there is often a listless and altogether vacant expression upon their faces; their eyes are black, and somewhat obliquely placed in their orbits. They have neither whiskers nor beard, their custom being to prevent them from growing by plucking them out on their first appearance. A vacant placidity, unmarked by strong emotions, is perhaps their predominant expression.

Of the five tribes mentioned, the Caribs are said to be the most numerous; brave, warlike, and industrious. They reside chiefly on the sea coast between the Essequebo and the Orinoco. It is from them that we get the name of the "Carribean Sea."

The Warraus are said to be a short, hardy race of fishermen, inhabiting the low, wet, marshy places adjacent to the sea. They are noted for their boat-building. They live on crabs and fish. In colour they are somewhat darker than the others. Their manners are bold, adventurous, and active. They are very improvident, and inclined to dissipation. Their features are irregular and disproportionate, the females being peculiarly disagreeable.

The Macoosi are famed for their manufacture of the Wourali poison. But the use of the poisoned

INDIAN WOMAN, WITH HAMMOCK AND PEGALL.

arrow is common to all these tribes, and Bancroft gives the recipe by which the Accawais arrow poison is usually prepared.

The Macoosi occupy the open savannahs of the Rupununi and Barima. They are described as inoffensive, taciturn, hospitable, and industrious. They are a numerous tribe, and are said to be implacable in their revenge. The picture before you is of a Macoosi Indian woman, travelling across the country in native costume. Her hammock is tied up, and she is carrying it upon her head. In it she rests by day and sleeps by night. On her back is what is called a pegall, in which she carries whatever may be needed on the way. In the basket at her feet, the cassava from the field is often carried, as well as pines and other kinds of vegetable produce. The only covering these natives wear is the little apron, manufactured by their own hands out of cotton thread grown in the forest and ornamented with different kinds of beads, variously coloured. The patterns of these dresses, if such they can be called, are beautiful and ingenious. They are red and blue and white. The fashion is not by any means modern, but it is serviceable and very ancient. The name of this covering is "Queyou."

The Accawais are the most interior tribe, living

near the source of the rivers Essequebo, Demerara, and Berbice. Dalton describes them as "of a nomadic, warlike nature, and wandering from the Orinoco to the Amazon, they engage in barter or battle with the other Indians according to circumstances." Their numbers are large, and their quarrelsome temper well known. They are disliked by the other tribes and have little if any communication with Europeans. Their complexion is lighter than the Warraus, and their features less disagreeable. "Their behaviour is reserved and grave, and they have an unusual degree of art and cunning. Their language is solemn and its articulations distinct but harsh. The arrow poison which they compound is particularly fatal; and besides that they have several other kinds of poison, which given in the smallest quantities, produces a very slow, but inevitable death. They have a composition which resembles wheat flour, which they sometimes use to avenge past injuries that have been long neglected and thought to be forgotten. On these occasions they always feign an insensibility of the injury which they intend to revenge, and even repay it with services and acts of friendship, until they have destroyed all distrust and apprehension of danger. When this is effected they meet their victim at some festival and engage him to drink

GROUP OF ACCAWAIS INDIANS.

with them. They drink first themselves to obviate suspicion, and afterwards secretly drops the poison into the potion, which they have already concealed under their finger nails, which are unusually long " (Bancroft).

The picture at the beginning of this book is from a photograph of a group of the Accawais. They wear no clothing save a strip of linen or cotton cloth, either blue or white, around their loins. This is passed over a cord tied round the body above the hips, in such a way that one part hangs down the front, like an apron, six inches wide, and the other hangs behind like a single attenuated coat tail. This article of dress is called a "lap." On their shoulders they have a necklet of alligators' teeth, these creatures being very numerous at the sources of their rivers. Around the head of the chief is a circular band, about two inches wide, woven from the fibre of a tree. In the upper edge of this is fixed a great number of long feathers of different but gay colours, red, blue, green, yellow, black, white, which stand erect round the whole circumference of the head. It gives them a wild and fierce appearance. In their hands they hold the battle axe or war club, which is made out of a wood as hard and as heavy as iron. It is sharpened at the edge like an axe. They have also their bows and arrows. At one side is a pegall, and at the other a large, circular iron-plate on which they bake their cassava cake.

But the most interesting of the tribes mentioned are the Arawaacks. These are they that form the subjects of our Mission. They live up our rivers where the land is elevated, and are in close proximity to the old Dutch plantations. In days gone by they were often the allies of the white man, and rendered good service in times of insurrection. "They are of a middle stature, and well proportioned. In complexion they are whiter than any of the other tribes. Their features are regular and agreeable, their lips thin, their eyes black and sparkling." Their necks are short, and their ankles, hands and feet, particularly those of the women, remarkably small. In temper and disposition they are cheerful and humane. To Europeans they are disposed to be friendly. In all my dealings with them I have found them kind and gentle and hospitable.

Those in our mission have begun to wear garments. A single petticoat and a bodice becomes the robe of the females, and the men wear a flannel and a light pair of blue cotton trousers. Of course, when "parson" is not there, or they go to their fields to plant or dig cassava, they fall back upon their native Indian robes. Previous to the introduction of Christianity, and in those places where no mission exists, they still wander about with the "queyou" as their only covering. The belle amongst the Bokeens wears usually around her neck a string of beads, with a tiger's tooth, or the tooth of a cayman in the middle. The "queyous" are beautifully made and fringed, and around their arms is the usual cotton band. Their marriages are of the simplest kind. An agreement being arrived at between the young people and the parents, the marriage is celebrated by a feast and dancing. He happiest to she happiest completes the ceremony.

Having rested for a short time on the stump of a tree, till our baggage was got out of the canoes, we began to march, Indian file, along a narrow path through the forest. The chief sent half of the men in front, placing " parson " in the middle. He walked close behind me, and the rest brought up the rear. I noticed as we passed along how quick they were in detecting reptiles upon the ground and on the trees. Once the chief stopped and pointed to a tree some distance off. There, curled round one of the branches, was a huge snake. I should probably not have seen it had I passed close to it, for it was nearly the colour of the wood around which it was clinging. Their tread, too, was so soft and cat-like. It was like a person with bare feet walking on tip-toes. Afterwards, when some of them paid me a visit in town and came to my church, I was amused to see the way in which they walked up the aisle, they might have been treading on boiled eggs. The senses of these Indians are very acute. Their sight, hearing, and smell have become naturally keen, from their continual exercise in watching for and tracking game. The Arawaacks have been termed the tiger-men, on account of the skill they display in overcoming the jaguar or tiger of the forest and coast. Wandering through the forest afterwards, with only one or two of them, I noticed how at different points they would break a twig or bend down a leaf. By these broken sticks they found their way back through the labyrinth of trees; for in those forests it is very easy to get lost. You may wander for weeks and months, and still find no way out, but perish in the attempt. An old writer who had lived amongst the Indians many years, says, " They will tell how many men, women, and children have passed, where a stranger could only see faint and confused marks on the path before him ; and from the appearance of the track and the state of the weather, will tell the

SECOND GROWTH FOREST.

time that has elapsed since the footprints were made. When arriving at a settlement, I have been disappointed at the absence of the people. The Indians with me would examine the fire-place, the dust on the utensils that had been left, and the various paths leading from the place, and they would then tell me when the people left the house, and the direction in which they were gone."

Any one who has wandered through these tropical forests must have been impressed with the wealth and exuberance of vegetable life. Successive generations of trees are there standing and flourishing around. There is the old tree, with its mighty trunk and its outspreading branches. This we may call the "octogenarian." Then there is the one that comes after this, the son of the old man. He is full-grown, and still sturdy and vigorous. Then there are younger ones, about half or two-thirds grown. They are struggling to make a place for themselves, and to find room for their outspreading branches. Then there are the young saplings—the children, we might call them. These are very numerous, and only a small proportion of these survive the dangers and perils of juvenility and grow up to mature life. Everywhere are trees, plants, shrubs, minute mosses, growth, exuberance, life. You cannot put down your foot without crushing some beautiful flower or graceful plant. Impenetrable thickets here and there present themselves, for creeping parasites or pliant vines have entwined themselves around the stalwart trees, climbing up the trunks, running along the branches, interlacing, encircling, with a kind of voluptuous embrace, that insidiously sucks the strength of the woody giant, but gives beauty and romance to the scene. Some of these vines are thick and strong and leafless, and are called bushropes, others are slender and graceful and leafy, and sometimes rich with a beautiful lilac, or purple, or white, or red flower. They hang in festoons and form a kind of drapery. So enveloped sometimes is the tree and hidden by these Delilah-like plants, that you would think it was the tree itself that was in bloom. Through these thickets, along a narrow path which the axe or the cutlass has carved, we wend our way. The sun is shining bright outside, but his rays cannot penetrate this leafy gloom. Here and there he may shoot through the tree-tops a spray of light, making the leaves glisten and the dew-drops sparkle and the concealed floral treasures appear. A mysterious silence reigns around. It is not the silence of the mountain-top, nor the silence of mid-ocean, nor the silence of some ancient ruin, nor the silence of the grave. It is more like the silence of the Eternal: a silence that comes not from emptiness, but from the very fulness of life; for if you listen attentively you will hear a stifled sound, a continued murmur. The sap is running up the arteries of the trees and coursing through the veins, the leaves are inhaling the nitrogen from the air, the branches are waving their leafy plumes. Myriads of insects are crawling among the dead leaves on the floor; from the decayed trunks of trees issue thousands upon thousands of red and black ants, all in full regimentals and marching order. There is not a rotting branch but is the home or the workshop of some beetle, or lizard, or millipede, or worm. We are in great Nature's laboratory; it is a magazine of wonders—all Nature breathes. It is the breath of God and the breath of life.

When we had travelled some distance I heard a noise that seemed to me at first like some one felling a tree, then it sounded again like distant thunder. I looked at the chief in wonderment, and he smiled. Then saying something in Arawaack to one of the men behind, two of them departed a little distance from us, and having taken up two stout cudgels they struck in turn the fluted trunk of a yarruroo tree. It sounded like the beating of a huge drum. "The Indians at the settlement," said the chief, "will now know that we are coming." It is in this way they give warning of the approach of a stranger. We may call it the Arawaack's telephone.

To those who have never seen an Indian settlement, words will fail to describe it. All around is the great forest. A space has been cleared for the houses. These houses, or wigwams or *Benaabs* as we call them, are of different sizes and shapes, and are placed irregularly. They are very simple in their structure, and quite in keeping with the primitive nature of the occupants. From a photograph which was taken, I am able to present my readers with a true picture of an Indian benaab. It consists of upright posts driven into the ground. These are held at the top by cross beams; not a nail or wooden pin is used in the fastening of them—they are simply tied together by bush-ropes. The roof is thatched with dehalibani leaves. Having arrived at the settlement, I found some thirty or forty benaabs promiscuously fixed about. In the centre of this strange circle stood a little Indian chapel, made after the same fashion, and close by was "parson's" benaab. "This," said the chief, "we give to you; it is your house. We glad you come amongst us to

AN INDIAN SETTLEMENT.   [To face p. 244

tell us of the great Father's love." I thanked him, and thought no more can I sing those three lines of Wesley's hymn—

> "No foot of land do I possess,
> Nor cottage in this wilderness,
> A poor wayfaring man;"

for now I have a house, it is on freehold land, and is given to me in perpetuity. On entering my benaab I found it quite empty. What was I to do? No furniture up here; not even a chair or a table or a three-legged stool. Well, I had my hammock, and that was soon fixed up for me, and we managed to make a bench and table out of some logs of wood. Forgetting all about my past training in the habits of civilised life, I fell into native simplicity, and became content with a broiled fish from the creek and a bit of cassava cake. By and by we were able to improve on this, and the Indians would add a bush fowl, or a piece of labba, or even a joint of venison. Our first service was held about five o'clock. Little Indian children, *in puris naturalibus*, sat on the rude benches in front and the men and women behind. About one hundred and twenty assembled. They sang in a soft simple way the sweet songs of the Saviour, and then after the reading of Scripture the chief interpreted to them my simple exposition. This over, I was taken to the different benaabs, and introduced to the respective families. The inside of these houses is very funny. There is no furniture save a cooking pot, an iron plate, a few utensils for making cassava cake, and a hammock. Indeed, these latter are hung all about the place. Some we found resting in them as in the picture before you, and some were squatting on pieces of wood. As many as ten and twelve hammocks will be swung in one benaab. The Indian lies in it during the day and sleeps in it at night. It is his *vade mecum*. Besides this benaab in the picture is a plantain tree, with its splendid leaves two feet wide and eight or ten feet long, this in itself forming a splendid shade from the heat of the sun.

During the night the dogs keep watch, and invariably a little fire of dried sticks is kept burning in each house. The Indians seem to sleep with one eye open, for I heard them talking many a time during the night, and they were up and about some hours before daylight in the morning; indeed, they frequently set out, five or six of them together, about three o'clock in the morning on some distant journey or to hunt in the forest.

Each day we had service in our little chapel at 7 a.m.; then from ten to twelve I taught every one that came into my house; from two to four I taught the children to read some short passages in the Bible and to sing some of our simple hymns; in the evening we again closed with family prayers. Thus the days went by, and I learned to pity and to love these simple denizens of the Wilderness.

The Gresham Press
UNWIN BROTHERS,
WOKING AND LONDON

BOOKS FOR RECREATION AND STUDY

PUBLISHED BY
T. FISHER UNWIN,
11, PATERNOSTER
BUILDINGS, LON-
DON, E.C. . . . .

T. FISHER UNWIN, Publisher,

THE STORY OF THE NATIONS
A SERIES OF POPULAR HISTORIES.

Each Volume is furnished with Maps, Illustrations, and Index. Large Crown 8vo., fancy cloth, gold lettered, or Library Edition, dark cloth, burnished red top, **5s.** *each.—Or may be had in half Persian, cloth sides, gilt tops; Price on Application.*

1. **Rome.** By ARTHUR GILMAN, M.A.
2. **The Jews.** By Professor J. K. HOSMER.
3. **Germany.** By the Rev. S. BARING-GOULD.
4. **Carthage.** By Professor ALFRED J. CHURCH.
5. **Alexander's Empire.** By Prof. J. P. MAHAFFY.
6. **The Moors in Spain.** By STANLEY LANE-POOLE.
7. **Ancient Egypt.** By Prof. GEORGE RAWLINSON.
8. **Hungary.** By Prof. ARMINIUS VAMBERY.
9. **The Saracens.** By ARTHUR GILMAN, M.A.
10. **Ireland.** By the Hon. EMILY LAWLESS.
11. **Chaldea.** By ZENAIDE A. RAGOZIN.
12. **The Goths.** By HENRY BRADLEY.
13. **Assyria.** By ZENAIDE A. RAGOZIN.
14. **Turkey.** By STANLEY LANE-POOLE.
15. **Holland.** By Professor J. E. THOROLD ROGERS.
16. **Mediæval France.** By GUSTAVE MASSON.
17. **Persia.** By S. G. W. BENJAMIN.
18. **Phœnicia.** By Prof. GEORGE RAWLINSON.
19. **Media.** By ZENAIDE A. RAGOZIN.
20. **The Hansa Towns.** By HELEN ZIMMERN.
21. **Early Britain.** By Professor ALFRED J. CHURCH.
22. **The Barbary Corsairs.** By STANLEY LANE-POOLE.
23. **Russia.** By W. R. MORFILL.
24. **The Jews under the Roman Empire.** By W. D. MORRISON.
25. **Scotland.** By JOHN MACKINTOSH, LL.D.
26. **Switzerland.** By R. STEAD and LINA HUG.
27. **Mexico.** By SUSAN HALE.
28. **Portugal.** By H. MORSE STEPHENS.
29. **The Normans.** By SARAH ORNE JEWETT.
30. **The Byzantine Empire.** By C. W. C. OMAN, M.A.
31. **Sicily: Phœnician, Greek and Roman.** By the late E. A. FREEMAN.
32. **The Tuscan and Genoa Republics.** By BELLA DUFFY.
33. **Poland.** By W. R. MORFILL.
34. **Parthia.** By Prof. GEORGE RAWLINSON.
35. **The Australian Commonwealth.** By GREVILLE TREGARTHEN.
36. **Spain.** By H. E. WATTS.
37. **Japan.** By DAVID MURRAY, Ph.D.
38. **South Africa.** By GEORGE M. THEAL.
39. **Venice.** By the Hon. ALETHEA WIEL.
40. **The Crusades:** The Latin Kingdom of Jerusalem. By T. A. ARCHER and CHARLES L. KINGSFORD.
41. **Vedic India.** By ZENAIDE A. RAGOZIN.
42. **The West Indies and the Spanish Main.** By JAMES RODWAY, F.L.S.
43. **Bohemia.** By C. E. MAURICE.
44. **The Balkans.** By W. MILLER.
45. **Canada.** By Dr. BOURINOT.
46. **British India.** By R. W. FRAZER, LL.B.
47. **Modern France.** By ANDRÉ LE BON.
The Franks. By LEWIS SERGEANT, B.A.

"Such a universal history as the series will present us with in its completion will be a possession such as no country but our own can boast of. . . . Its success on the whole has been very remarkable."—*Daily Chronicle.*

11, Paternoster Buildings, London, E.C.

T. FISHER UNWIN, Publisher,

THE CHILDREN'S STUDY
• • •

Long 8vo., cloth, gilt top, with photogravure frontispiece, price **2/6** *each.*

1. **Scotland.** By Mrs. OLIPHANT.
2. **Ireland.** Edited by BARRY O'BRIEN.
3. **England.** By FRANCES E. COOKE.
4. **Germany.** By KATE FREILIGRATH KROEKER, Author of "Fairy Tales from Brentano," &c.
5. **Old Tales from Greece.** By ALICE ZIMMERN.
6. **France.** By MARY ROWSELL.
7. **The United States.** By MINNA SMITH.
8. **Rome.** By MARY FORD.

OPINIONS OF THE PRESS ON "SCOTLAND."

"For children of the right age this is an excellent little history."—*Daily News.*
"Enough of fault-finding with a writer who has otherwise performed his task in a perfectly charming manner."—*Daily Chronicle.*
"The best book for the rising Caledonian that has appeared for many a day."
"Simple, picturesque, and well-proportioned."—*Glasgow Herald.* [*Scotsman.*
"A charming book full of life and colour."—*Speaker.*
"As a stimulator of the imagination and intelligence, it is a long way ahead of many books in use in some schools."—*Sketch.*
"The book is attractively produced. Mrs. Oliphant has performed her difficult task well."—*Educational Times.*
"A work which may claim its place upon the shelves of the young people's library, where it may prove of not a little service also to their elders."—*School Board Chronicle.*

OPINIONS OF THE PRESS ON "IRELAND."

"Many who are children no longer will be glad of this compact but able introduction to the story of Ireland's woes. The form of the volume is particularly attractive."
British Weekly.
"We heartily congratulate Mr. Barry O'Brien upon this interesting little volume. The style is intensely interesting."—*Schoolmaster.*
"It is well that the youth of England, who have entered into a serious inheritance and who will soon be the voters of England, should have some conception of the country with whom they are so closely bound up, and for whose past their fathers are so heavily responsible. We do not know of any work so fitting for imparting to them this knowledge as the present, which, therefore, we heartily commend to all teachers as the best text-book of Irish history for the young."—*Daily Chronicle.*

OPINIONS OF THE PRESS ON "ENGLAND."

"Terse, vivid, well-informed."—*Speaker.*
"Pleasantly written, and well within the capacity of a young child. . . . We anticipate with pleasure the appearance of the succeeding volumes of 'The Children's Study.'"—*School Guardian.*
"Admirably done . . . . always easy of understanding."—*Scotsman.*

OPINIONS OF THE PRESS ON "GERMANY."

"We have seldom seen a small history so well balanced, and consequently so adequate as an introduction to the subject."—*Educational Times.*
"Painstaking and well written."—*Daily Chronicle.*
"Clear as accurate. It is just the sort of book to give to a youngster who has to study Teutonic history."—*Black and White.*
"An interesting historical series."—*Pall Mall Gazette.*

11, Paternoster Buildings, London, E.C.

T. FISHER UNWIN, Publisher,

BUILDERS OF GREATER BRITAIN

EDITED BY

H. F. WILSON

A Set of 10 Volumes, each with Photogravure Frontispiece, and Map, large crown 8vo., cloth, 5s. each.

The completion of the Sixtieth year of the Queen's reign will be the occasion of much retrospect and review, in the course of which the great men who, under the auspices of Her Majesty and her predecessors, have helped to make the British Empire what it is to-day, will naturally be brought to mind. Hence the idea of the present series. These biographies, concise but full, popular but authoritative, have been designed with the view of giving in each case an adequate picture of the builder in relation to his work.

The series will be under the general editorship of Mr. H. F. Wilson, formerly Fellow of Trinity College, Cambridge, and now private secretary to the Right Hon. J. Chamberlain at the Colonial Office. Each volume will be placed in competent hands, and will contain the best portrait obtainable of its subject, and a map showing his special contribution to the Imperial edifice. The first to appear will be a Life of Sir Walter Ralegh, by Major Hume, the learned author of "The Year after the Armada." Others in contemplation will deal with the Cabots, the quarter-centenary of whose sailing from Bristol is has recently been celebrated in that city, as well as in Canada and Newfoundland; Sir Thomas Maitland, the "King Tom" of the Mediterranean; Rajah Brooke, Sir Stamford Raffles, Lord Clive, Edward Gibbon Wakefield, Zachary Macaulay, &c., &c.

The Series has taken for its motto the Miltonic prayer:—

"𝕿𝖍𝖔𝖚 𝖂𝖍𝖔 𝖔𝖋 𝕿𝖍𝖞 𝖋𝖗𝖊𝖊 𝖌𝖗𝖆𝖈𝖊 𝖉𝖎𝖉𝖘𝖙 𝖇𝖚𝖎𝖑𝖉 𝖚𝖕 𝖙𝖍𝖎𝖘 𝕭𝖗𝖎𝖙𝖙𝖆𝖓𝖓𝖎𝖈𝖐 𝕰𝖒𝖕𝖎𝖗𝖊 𝖙𝖔 𝖆 𝖌𝖑𝖔𝖗𝖎𝖔𝖚𝖘 𝖆𝖓𝖉 𝖊𝖓𝖛𝖎𝖆𝖇𝖑𝖊 𝖍𝖊𝖎𝖌𝖍𝖙𝖍. 𝖂𝖎𝖙𝖍 𝖆𝖑𝖑 𝖍𝖊𝖗 𝕯𝖆𝖚𝖌𝖍𝖙𝖊𝖗 𝕴𝖘𝖑𝖆𝖓𝖉𝖘 𝖆𝖇𝖔𝖚𝖙 𝖍𝖊𝖗, 𝖘𝖙𝖆𝖞 𝖚𝖘 𝖎𝖓 𝖙𝖍𝖎𝖘 𝖋𝖊𝖑𝖎𝖈𝖎𝖙𝖎𝖊."

1. **SIR WALTER RALEGH.** By MARTIN A. S. HUME, Author of "The Courtships of Queen Elizabeth," &c.

2. **SIR THOMAS MAITLAND;** the Mastery of the Mediterranean. By WALTER FREWEN LORD.

3. **JOHN CABOT AND HIS SONS;** the Discovery of North America. By C. RAYMOND BEAZLEY, M.A.

4. **LORD CLIVE;** the Foundation of British Rule in India. By Sir A. J. ARBUTHNOT, K.C.S.I., C.I.E.

5. **EDWARD GIBBON WAKEFIELD;** the Colonisation of South Australia and New Zealand. By R. GARNETT, C.B., LL.D.

6. **RAJAH BROOKE;** the Englishman as Ruler of an Eastern State. By Sir SPENSER ST. JOHN, G.C.M.G.

7. **ADMIRAL PHILIP;** the Founding of New South Wales. By LOUIS BECKE and WALTER JEFFERY.

8. **SIR STAMFORD RAFFLES;** England in the Far East. By the Editor.

T. FISHER UNWIN, Publisher,

THE ADVENTURE SERIES
POPULAR RE-ISSUE.

Each large crown 8vo., fully illustrated. Popular re-issue, **3s. 6d.** *per vol. ; in two styles of binding, viz., decorative cover, cut edges ; and plain library style, untouched edges.*

1. **Adventures of a Younger Son.** By EDWARD J. TRELAWNEY. Introduction by EDWARD GARNETT.

2. **Madagascar;** or, Robert Drury's Journal during his Captivity on that Island. Preface and Notes by Captain S. P. OLIVER, R.A.

3. **Memoirs of the Extraordinary Military Career of John Shipp.**

4. **The Buccaneers and Marooners of America.** Edited and Illustrated by HOWARD PYLE.

5. **The Log of a Jack Tar:** Being the Life of James Choyce, Master Mariner. Edited by Commander V. LOVETT CAMERON.

6. **Ferdinand Mendez Pinto, the Portuguese Adventurer.** New Edition. Annotated by Prof. A. VAMBÉRY.

7. **Adventures of a Blockade Runner.** By WILLIAM WATSON. Illustrated by ARTHUR BYNG, R.N.

SOME PRESS NOTICES.

"In the excellent ADVENTURE SERIES, not only are old tales of adventure retold but new tales are brought to men's ears."—*Scotsman.*
"One of the most entertaining collections of the kind ever published."—*Echo.*
"This unique set of volumes."—*Daily Chronicle.*
"An interesting series."—*St. James's Gazette.*
"The whole series has been of exceptional interest."—*Cape Argus.*
"Amply fulfils its purpose by showing that the taste for stories of adventure may be gratified by narratives of fact without resorting to the ingenious absurdities of modern fiction."—*Literary World.*
"That interesting series."—*Schoolmaster.*

11, Paternoster Buildings, London, E.C.

SOME WORKS BY REV. E. J. HARDY

"The Murray of Matrimony, the Baedeker of Bliss."

HOW TO BE HAPPY THOUGH MARRIED

Popular Edition, gilt edges, cloth, bevelled boards, **3s. 6d.**
Presentation Edition, white vellum, cloth, bevelled boards, gilt edges, in box, **7s. 6d.**

"An entertaining volume. . . . The new guide to matrimonial felicity."—*Standard.*
"This charming volume. . . . Wit and wisdom abound in its pages; as for the good stories, they are almost too plentiful."—*Spectator.*

Uniform in style and prices with the foregoing.

THE FIVE TALENTS OF WOMAN
A Book for Girls and Young Women

THE BUSINESS OF LIFE
A Book for Everyone

Square imperial 16mo., cloth, **3s. 6d.**—*Presentation Edition, bevelled boards, gilt edges, in box,* **7s. 6d.**

"Calculated to teach the art of happiness and contentment as well as mere exhortation can teach it."—*Times.*
"Pleasant as well as profitable reading."—*Literary World.*
"A host of social subjects are treated in a way at once wise and witty, and in a manner as delightful to read as they are pleasantly 'improving.'"—*Daily Telegraph.*

THE SUNNY DAYS OF YOUTH
A Book for Boys and Young Men

Square Imperial 16mo., cloth, **3s. 6d.**—*Presentation Edition, elegantly bound, bevelled boards, gilt edges,* **7s. 6d.**

"It is an excellent book for a serious-minded boy."—*Scotsman.*
"The pleasantest reading possible . . . this useful little book."—*Educational Review.*
"As well written as it is unquestionably well-intentioned."—*Leeds Mercury.*

FAINT YET PURSUING

Square Imperial 16mo. Popular Edition. Crown 8vo., cloth, **3s. 6d.**

"Will meet with an extensive recognition."—*Morning Post.*
"Short and sensible . . . they form fresh and breezy reading."—*Glasgow Herald.*

"MANNERS MAKYTH MAN"

Presentation Edition, imperial 16mo., cloth, bevelled boards, in box, **7s. 6d.**; cloth, **6s.** Popular Edition, small square 8vo., cloth, **3s. 6d.**

"Good-natured, wholesome, and straightforward."—*Saturday Review.*
"A really delightful volume, well adapted for family reading."—*Christian World.*

THE LOVES OF SOME FAMOUS MEN
Imperial 16mo., cloth, **6s.**

T. FISHER UNWIN, Publisher,

WORKS BY PROF. PASQUALE VILLARI

THE LIFE AND TIMES OF GIROLAMO SAVONAROLA

Translated by LINDA VILLARI

New and Cheaper Edition in one volume. Fully Illustrated.
Cloth, large crown, **7s. 6d.**

" No more interesting book has been issued during the present season."
Pall Mall Gazette.
"The most interesting religious biography that we know of in modern times."
Spectator.
" A book which is not likely to be forgotten."—*Athenæum.*
" By far the best book on Savonarola available for English readers."—*Standard.*
" Is perhaps *the* book of the publishing season."—*Star.*
"Sincere, complete, and, upon the whole, well-balanced and candid."—*Yorkshire Post.*
" A work of very great value."—*Scotsman.*
"No more graphic view of the ecclesiastical and social life of ancient Italy has been opened up for us than this of Linda Villari."—*Morning Leader.*
" As complete and trustworthy as care, judgment, and the fullest investigation can make it."—*Dundee Advertiser.*
" A credit to the publisher."—*Independent.*

THE LIFE AND TIMES OF NICCOLÒ MACHIAVELLI

2 Vols., 8vo., with Illustrations, **32s.**

"Indispensable to the serious student of Machiavelli, his teaching and his times."
Times.
"The fullest and most authoritative history of Machiavelli and his times ever given to the British public."—*Glasgow Herald.*
" May be regarded as an authority on the times of which it treats. . . . The book is enriched with rare and interesting illustrations, and with some valuable historical documents."—*Daily Telegraph.*

THE TWO FIRST CENTURIES OF FLORENTINE HISTORY

2 Vols., with Illustrations, 8vo., **16s.** *each.*

" Professor Villari's learned and original work. . . . Its value has long been recognised by all competent students of Dante and of the Florentine history of his time."—*Times.*
" Its value to those in search of real knowledge could not be easily exaggerated."
Scotsman.

11, Paternoster Buildings, London, E.C.

T. FISHER UNWIN, Publisher,

THE CENTURY DICTIONARY

Six volumes bound in cloth, gilt lettered, sprinkled edges,
per vol. **£2 2s.**
Do. in half morocco, marbled edges, per vol. **£2 16s.**
24 Parts, strongly bound in cloth, per part, **10s. 6d.**
BOOKCASE for holding the Dictionary, price **£3 3s.**

Size of each volume 13 in. × 9¼ in. × 2¼ in.

PRESS NOTICES.

"The exceptional merits of the 'Century Dictionary' are beyond dispute."—*Times.*

"One of the most notable monuments of the philological industry of the age."
—*Daily Telegraph.*

"It is a work of great ability, fine scholarship, and patient research in many widely different departments of learning."—*Standard.*

"As we turn the leaves of this splendid work, we feel acutely the inadequacy of any description apart from actual handling of the volumes."—*Daily Chronicle.*

"It is fuller, more complete, with fewer faults than any rival."—*Pall Mall Gazette.*

THE CYCLOPÆDIA OF NAMES

Cloth, **£2 2s.** net.; half morocco, **£2 15s.** net.

Size—13 in. × 9¼ × 2¼ in.

PRESS NOTICES.

"A book of ready reference for proper names of every conceivable kind."—*Daily News.*

"The 'Cyclopædia of Names' deserves to rank with important works of reference, for though its facts on any given subject are, of course, elementary, they can be quickly found, and, on the whole, they are admirably chosen."—*Standard.*

"A most handsome and solid volume . . . . It will be found exceedingly useful. . . It is beautifully printed."—*Daily Chronicle.*

"A most valuable compilation, and one which will be valued for the great mass of information which it contains."—*Glasgow Herald.*

"Every library of reference, no matter how richly stocked, will be the richer for having it . . . . may be consulted freely without the inconveniences of human haulage."—*Scotsman.*

11, Paternoster Buildings, London, E.C.

T. FISHER UNWIN, Publisher,

SOME 3/6 NOVELS

Uniform Edition of MARK RUTHERFORD'S works. Edited by REUBEN SHAPCOTT. Crown 8vo., cloth.

The Autobiography of Mark Rutherford. Fifth Edition.

Mark Rutherford's Deliverance. New Edition.

Miriam's Schooling, and other Papers. By MARK RUTHERFORD. With Frontispiece by WALTER CRANE. Second Edition.

The Revolution in Tanner's Lane.

Catharine Furze: A Novel. By MARK RUTHERFORD. Fourth Edition.

Clara Hopgood. By MARK RUTHERFORD.

"These writings are certainly not to be lightly dismissed, bearing as they do the impress of a mind which, although limited in range and sympathies, is decidedly original."—*Times.*

The Statement of Stella Maberly. By F. ANSTEY, Author of "Vice Versâ." Crown 8vo. cloth.
"It is certainly a strange and striking story."—*Athenæum.*

Ginette's Happiness. Being a translation by RALPH DERECHEF of "Le Bonheur de Ginette." Crown 8vo., cloth.
"Pretty and gracefully told."—*Pall Mall Gazette.*

Silent Gods and Sun-Steeped Lands. By R. W. FRAZER. Second Edition. With 4 full-page Illustrations by A. D. MCCORMICK and a Photogravure Frontispiece. Small crown 8vo., cloth.
"Mr. Frazer writes powerfully and well, and seems to have an intimate acquaintance with the sun-steeped land, and the strange beings who people it."—*Glasgow Herald.*

Paul Heinsius. By CORA LYSTER. Crown 8vo., cloth.
"This is an extremely clever and altogether admirable, but not altogether unkindly, anatomisation of Teutonic character."—*Daily Chronicle.*

My Bagdad. By ELLIOTT DICKSON. Illustrated. 8vo., cloth.
"Related with a refreshing simplicity that is certain to approve itself to readers."—*Bookseller.*

Silk of the Kine. By L. MCMANUS (C. MacGuire), Author of "Amabel: A Military Romance." Crown 8vo., cloth.
"We have read 'The Silk of the Kine,' from the first page to the last, without missing a single word, and we sighed regretfully when Mr. McManus brought the adventures of Margery MacGuire and Piers Ottley to a close."—*Literary World.*

A Pot of Honey. By SUSAN CHRISTIAN. Crown 8vo., cloth.
"The book is the outcome of a clever mind."—*Athenæum.*

Liza of Lambeth. By W. SOMERSET MAUGHAM. Crown 8vo., cloth.
"An interesting story of life and character in the Surrey-side slums, presented with a great deal of sympathetic humour."—*Daily Chronicle.*

The Twilight Reef, and other Stories. By HERBERT C. MCILWAINE. Crown 8vo., cloth.

11, Paternoster Buildings, London, E.C.

T. FISHER UNWIN, Publisher,

THE MERMAID SERIES

The Best Plays of the Old Dramatists
Literal Reproductions of the Old Text.

Post 8vo., each Volume containing about 500 pages, and an etched Frontispiece, cloth, **3s. 6d.** *each.*

1. **The Best Plays of Christopher Marlowe.** Edited by HAVELOCK ELLIS, and containing a General Introduction to the Series by JOHN ADDINGTON SYMONDS.

2. **The Best Plays of Thomas Otway.** Introduction by the Hon. RODEN NOEL.

3. **The Best Plays of John Ford.**—Edited by HAVELOCK ELLIS.

4 and 5. **The Best Plays of Thomas Massinger.** Essay and Notes by ARTHUR SYMONS.

6. **The Best Plays of Thomas Heywood.** Edited by A. W. VERITY. Introduction by J. A. SYMONDS.

7. **The Complete Plays of William Wycherley.** Edited by W. C. WARD.

8. **Nero, and other Plays.** Edited by H. P. HORNE, ARTHUR SYMONS, A. W. VERITY, and H. ELLIS.

9 and 10. **The Best Plays of Beaumont and Fletcher.** Introduction by J. ST. LOE STRACHEY.

11. **The Complete Plays of William Congreve.** Edited by ALEX. C. EWALD.

12. **The Best Plays of Webster and Tourneur.** Introduction by JOHN ADDINGTON SYMONDS.

13 and 14. **The Best Plays of Thomas Middleton.** Introduction by ALGERNON CHARLES SWINBURNE

15. **The Best Plays of James Shirley.** Introduction by EDMUND GOSSE.

16. **The Best Plays of Thomas Dekker.** Notes by ERNEST RHYS.

17, 19, and 20. **The Best Plays of Ben Jonson.** Vol. I. edited, with Introduction and Notes, by BRINSLEY NICHOLSON and C. H. HERFORD.

18. **The Complete Plays of Richard Steele.** Edited, with Introduction and Notes, by G. A. AITKEN.

21. **The Best Plays of George Chapman.** Edited by WILLIAM LYON PHELPS, Instructor of English Literature at Yale College.

22. **The Select Plays of Sir John Vanbrugh.** Edited, with an Introduction and Notes, by A. E. H. SWAEN.

PRESS OPINIONS.

"Even the professed scholar with a good library at his command will find some texts here not otherwise easily accessible; while the humbler student of slender resources, who knows the bitterness of not being able to possess himself of the treasure stored in expensive folios or quartos long out of print, will assuredly rise up and thank Mr. Unwin."—*St. James's Gazette.*

"Resumed under good auspices."—*Saturday Review.*

"The issue is as good as it could be."—*British Weekly.*

"At once scholarly and interesting."—*Leeds Mercury.*

11, Paternoster Buildings, London, E.C.

www.ingramcontent.com/pod-product-compliance
Lightning Source LLC
Chambersburg PA
CBHW031903220426
43663CB00006B/747